BLAIR HILL AND HIGHLANDS
on Moosehead Lake

BLAIR HILL AND HIGHLANDS
on Moosehead Lake
A History

SEAN D. BILLINGS AND JOHANNA S. BILLINGS

THE
History
PRESS

Published by The History Press
Charleston, SC
www.historypress.com

First published 2024

Manufactured in the United States

ISBN 9781467154727

Library of Congress Control Number: 2024931503

Notice: The information in this book is true and complete to the best of our knowledge. It is offered without guarantee on the part of the authors or The History Press. The authors and The History Press disclaim all liability in connection with the use of this book.

To the women of Blair Hill, past and present.

CONTENTS

ACKNOWLEDGEMENTS

The Moosehead Lake Historical Society played a critical role in assisting us with the research for this book. We would like to extend special thanks to Suzanne M. AuClair, Candy Russell, Mary Stefanik, Andrea Johns and Barbara Crossman for their enthusiastic support for this project. The historical society not only provided some of the documents used to research this book but also offered encouragement and appreciation for our efforts. When we discovered, for example, that many of the people who played significant roles in the history of Greenville were connected through their Chicago Board of Trade, the historical society invited Sean to write articles about these findings. Such appreciation and encouragement was highly motivating and made us feel good about the project. It's nice to know our work is appreciated.

Although the historical society was an important hub for our research, it was not the only one. We sought to find as many people as possible who had knowledge of the Blair Hill area. In addition to information, these conversations allowed us to make friends and better know those living nearby. As such, we would like to thank the following people for their support. Listed in no particular order: Dan and Ruth McLaughlin and Jennifer Whitlow for information on Blair Hill Inn; Ed and Arlene Jewett and Josh Wallace for information on The Cottages; David Tozier for information on the Moosehead Coffee House; Linda Koski for information on the Scammon farm; Prudy Tornquist Richards for background on the Tornquist family; Edmund Bigney for information on the Scammon and Bigney families;

Rocky and Stephanie Elsemore for information on the Elsemore family; Karl Watler for information on the Horizons West development; Stephen and Suzanne Foster for information on the Macfarlane House; and Dave Hall and Jessica Hall for information on the Hall family.

Of course, we must also thank Arcadia Publishing for believing in the project enough to publish it. Having the backing of a publisher will allow us to reach a larger audience than we could on our own.

INTRODUCTION

Moosehead Lake is the largest lake in Maine and the largest mountain lake in the eastern United States. Located in the center of the Maine Highlands Region, the lake is forty miles long and covers nearly seventy-five thousand acres. Naturally, a lake of this size attracts people. Many of the early visitors came for vacation. Others wanted to move here permanently or at least stay for the whole summer. Greenville became the gateway to the lake because of its location at the southern end and its being the last village before the North Woods. Articles in early travel guides show that what later became known as Blair Hill was famous for its spectacular views.

This book covers Blair Hill and the Highlands area from Hall Avenue up the hill to the area of Shoals Road. It covers town lots 80, 81, 82, 85, 86, 87, 88, 89, 90, 91 and 92 as shown on the original plan of the Saco Free Bridge property. Lots 80 to 87 were originally owned by Edmund Scammon, then by Victor Macfarlane and then by the Sloper family. Lots 88 to 92 belonged to the Shaws and Youngs and eventually came under the ownership of the Halls.

We became interested in the history of this area after we purchased our home on Lily Bay Road. The house had been built as a camp by Michael and Ellen L. Jobin when Ellen owned the Blair Mansion. We are surrounded by woods and what seemed to be an unspoiled piece of nature. However, while exploring the woods behind our house, we discovered stone walls and barbed wire running through our property along with a one-inch steel pipe.

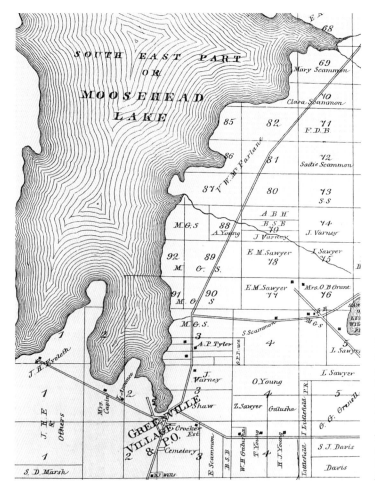

This map from the 1882 Atlas of Piscataquis County, Maine, shows the locations of lots 79 through 93, which are the main focus of this book. *Courtesy Ed Jewett.*

Barbed wire is typically used for keeping farm animals in or out of an area, and since most settlers in the 1800s had to rely on some type of farming to survive, that made sense. The pipe was a bit of a mystery, though. Further investigation revealed that the pipe terminates at the ruins of a springhouse that served as a water source for the Scammon farm and, possibly, as a public water trough along what is now Lily Bay Road. The spring flows continually, even at temperatures of negative twenty and in drought conditions. When Erwin Sloper was subdividing the land in 1948, his plan set aside the spring with about two acres of land, calling it the "Spring Lot."

We began looking for old postcards of the area, hoping to find a photograph of the springhouse. Although we didn't succeed in that endeavor, we found numerous cards showing the Moosehead Coffee

House, the Highlands, Macfarlane House, Greenslope, Hillside Gardens and the Blair Mansion. These postcards piqued our interest and spurred further research, which showed the histories of these different places were actually tied together.

The Macfarlanes owned property in Greenville starting in 1872 but lived in Chicago. Lyman Blair of Chicago married Cornelia Macfarlane, and they moved to Greenville. The Blairs built a mansion overlooking the Macfarlane House and lake, and this would become the Blair Hill Inn. Macfarlane sold the remaining land to Andrew J. Sloper and his two sons, Harold and William. Andrew would build Greenslope for his second wife, Myra, and this would become the Lodge at Moosehead Lake. Andrew and Myra had another son, Erwin, who would eventually control most of the property and begin developing it. His work set in motion the events that would give rise to other camps and lodges, including The Cottages and Moosehead Lodge. This area on the hill right outside the Village of Greenville became a popular vacation spot, and lodges, sporting camps and housekeeping cottages appeared among the larger homes owned by Macfarlane, Blair and, later, the Slopers. Ironically, most of the small lodges, sporting camps and housekeeping cottages have become private residences or private summer cottages, and the large homes of people like Blair and the Slopers have become upscale inns and lodges.

All the properties detailed in this book are privately owned. The properties that are now inns are open only to their guests and patrons, so please respect private property.

In the course of our research, naturally we learned about the men who built this part of Greenville and, by extension, the women in their lives. Because of the customs and laws of the past, history emphasizes the contributions of the men, giving the women only a cursory mention, if any. We chose to dedicate the book to the women of Blair Hill because, without them, the area would not have become what it is today.

For example, Sarah Scammon came to the area in 1831 with her husband and seven children before the town of Greenville even existed. At that time, there were only a few dozen residents. Even with modern-day conveniences, few people would be willing to relocate to the wilderness and care for seven children.

There are many more examples. Emma Cameron handled much of the legal and financial affairs for her family, including the mortgage for the sale of the Scammon farm to Victor Macfarlane. Zanina Macfarlane purchased the mortgage that Emma Cameron held against Victor Macfarlane to ensure

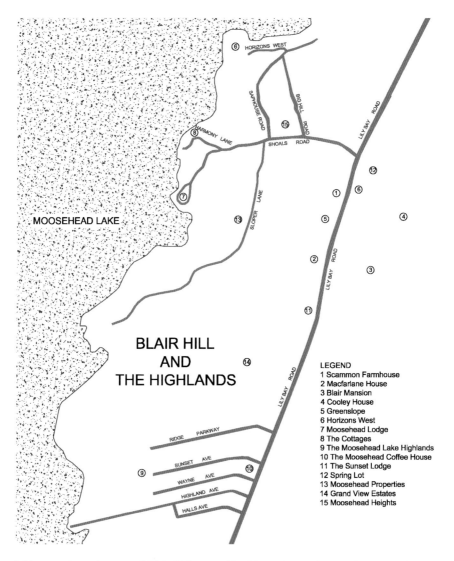

This map shows the area of Blair Hill covered in this book as well as the locations of the properties discussed. *Illustration by Sean Billings.*

the property remained safe. Cornelia Macfarlane Blair was also active in the financial dealings of her husband and father. In 1907, when the veneer mill was going bankrupt, she foreclosed on a mortgage she held on her father's personal property, keeping the property from being taken to settle debts. Edith M. Barney owned and operated the Moosehead Coffee House and made it one of the most famous restaurants in the area at the time. Carlotta

Sloper, May Butterworth, Roberta Johnson Nicholas, Acelia Hall and Harmony Cheyney all had lasting effects on the legacy of Blair Hill.

These are just a few of the colorful and strong women who shaped this part of Greenville. Each deserves more space than we have in this book, so we encourage everyone to pick up where we left off with this research and discover more of their stories.

Chapter 1

THE ORIGINAL SCAMMON FARMHOUSE

The history of the Scammon farm stretches all the way back to the early 1800s, before the town of Greenville existed. It encompasses the area where the Blair Hill Inn is currently situated as well as the properties on the other side of what is now Lily Bay Road, where tourists are known to stop to enjoy the view. The Scammon farm was, of course, much bigger than that, but these landmarks are situated near where the original farmhouse once stood.

Greenville was first surveyed as "Township Nine and Range Ten." During this period, land grants were given to groups or communities that could then sell the land for profit or settle on it. The township was formed by a public grant from Massachusetts around 1812 and was divided into northern and southern sections. The southern part of the township was granted to Thornton Academy in Saco and contained approximately eleven thousand acres. It was purchased by Nathaniel Haskell in 1824. The northern part, which is the subject of this book, was granted to an organization called the Saco Free Bridge. The line between the northern and southern sections would have been slightly north of present-day Scammon Road and parallel to that road eastward, through both Sawyer Pond and Wilson Pond.

The northern section was surveyed in 1830 by H.K. Stanton and divided into one-hundred-acre rectangular lots, numbered from 1 to 93. In 1829, these lots were sold off to a number of buyers, including the Sawyers, Shaws, Tufts and Coles. Having purchased lots 81, 82 and 85 of the original Stanton survey, Edmund Scammon moved to the area from

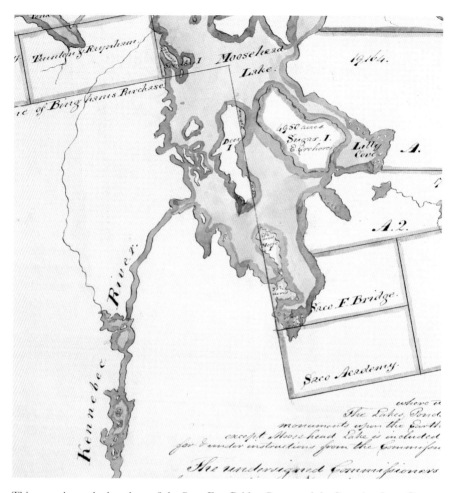

This map shows the locations of the Saco Free Bridge Grant and the Saco Academy Grant, which make up present-day Greenville. All properties covered in this book are located within the Saco Free Bridge Grant. *Authors' collection.*

Saco with his wife, Sarah (Haley), and their seven children, Mary, Robert, Hannah, Edmund, Daniel, Samuel and Lydia. They arrived in 1831, five years before the town of Greenville was incorporated in 1836 and seventy-eight years before Lily Bay Road was officially constructed. Interestingly, three of Scammon's children died relatively young. Robert died in 1847 at the age of thirty-six, Hannah died in 1844 at the age of thirty and Daniel died in 1839 at the age of twenty-one.

A rough road was cut to the Scammon property from the Haskell settlement, which was located near the present Greenville airport. It

This tintype photo shows Edmund Scammon Jr., who came to Greenville in 1831 with his parents, Edmund and Sarah Scammon, and his brother and sisters. Edmund Jr. never married. The Scammons were originally from Saco. *Collection of the Moosehead Historical Society, accession number 2010.15.0078.*

followed much the same path as the existing Varney Road, going past Sawyer Pond and out Higgins Road. It was used for many years, but at some point, it was replaced by what we now know as Lily Bay Road. An 1858 map of Piscataquis shows a road in the same location of the present Lily Bay Road that ended at the Scammon farm. At this time, the old road that went past the Sawyer farm ended before going through to the Scammon farm at a spot labeled "Canadians." Maps put out in 1874 and 1880 by John M. Way Jr. for his *Moosehead Lake and the Headwaters of the Penobscot & St. John Rivers* and Thomas Sedgwick Steele's *Canoe and Camera* show Lily Bay Road going past the Scammon farm and out into the North Woods. In 1919, the road from Greenville to Lily Bay was built—or rebuilt, depending on your definition—by the Great Northern Paper Company.

While they cleared the land and built what was to become their farm, the Scammons spent their first year in the Haskell cabin, which was within walking distance of their land.

Edmund, who was born in 1780, died on February 4, 1837, and this was Greenville's first recorded death. His wife, Sarah, who was born in 1785, died on May 22, 1858. After the senior Edmund's death, three of his children sold their shares of the property to their brother Edmund Jr. Robert did so in 1837, Samuel in 1854 and Mary in 1856.

The Scammon farm was still standing in 1936, and the buildings were the second oldest in Greenville, according to the *History of Greenville* by Emma J. True, published that year.

In an interview, Edmund Bigney, who is one of Scammon's descendants, said hay was one of the primary crops raised by the Scammons, both on Edmund's farm and on one owned by his brother, Samuel Scammon, on Scammon Road. They sold the hay to the logging companies to feed the oxen and horses used when harvesting timber. Bigney also stated that Edmund had a road on his property down to the lake, possibly around the location of Shoals Road, to a place that at that time was called Scammon

Landing. There, hay was loaded onto boats and shipped up the lake to the logging companies.

Census data for 1850 shows Edmund Scammon Jr. living in Greenville and working as a farmer and lumberman. The 1880 census lists him as having a single occupation as a lumberman. When he sold the original Scammon farm, Edmund Jr. must have given up farming to concentrate on lumbering. He died on November 30, 1881. He must have been a successful lumberman because the 1882 Piscataquis Atlas shows his estate owning most of the northern part of Greenville, consisting of thirty-five lots or about 3,500 acres.

On September 12, 1865, Edmund Jr. sold his farm, which consisted of lots 80, 81, 82, 85 and 86 and containing about 450 acres, to James Cameron and his wife, Emma, of Nashville, Tennessee, for $1,000.

James Cameron was a portrait and landscape painter. Some of his work is in the permanent collection of the Hunter Museum of Art in Chattanooga, Tennessee. He also did the original artwork for some of the Currier and Ives lithographs. The Amon Carter Museum of American Art in Fort Worth, Texas, has some of these lithographs in its collection.

James was born on September 19, 1816, in Greenock, Renfrewshire, Scotland, son of Dr. William and Agnes Cameron. In 1833, he moved with his family to the Mantua section of Philadelphia, where he studied art. By

The Scammon farm was located at the far northern end of Lily Bay Road. The road ended at the barn, as shown here. The Scammon farm overlooked Moosehead Lake, and the property contained around 450 acres. *Collection of the Moosehead Historical Society, accession number 2011.106.0004.*

1839, he was living in Indianapolis, Indiana, and was an active portrait painter. In 1840, he moved back to Philadelphia, but by 1842, he was in St. Louis, Missouri, where he achieved success as a portrait painter.

In 1842, while preparing for his trip to St. Louis, he befriended his neighbor, seventeen-year-old Emma S. Alcock. This turned into more than friendship, and they announced their engagement in September 1843, marrying on March 5, 1844. After their wedding, they toured Italy and enjoyed a three-year residency there. The Camerons returned to Philadelphia in 1848. In July 1851, they moved to Washington, D.C., in an effort to restart James's painting career in the United States. Over the next few years, the Camerons bounced from Washington, D.C., to Philadelphia and to the Adirondacks in New York State.

In 1856, the Camerons moved to Knoxville, Tennessee, where James met Colonel James A. Whiteside of Chattanooga, a leader in the legislature. James did portraits of the Whiteside family, and in 1858, Whiteside encouraged the Camerons to stay in Chattanooga by selling them property now known as Cameron Hill. On December 16, 1859, the Camerons began building their farm on the property. During the Civil War, the Camerons remained pro-Union, and at one point the Union army took control of Cameron Hill, using it as a fort and camp. The Camerons were compensated after the war for the woods, orchards and buildings that had been destroyed by the army.

After the war, the Camerons began selling off the Cameron Hill property. James went into business, but his firm, Cameron, Grier and Co., was not successful. James still wanted to paint landscapes, and moving to Moosehead Lake seems like something that would inspire this. Instead of painting, however, James became a minister, serving at the Union Church in Greenville from 1869 until June 30, 1871. The Camerons owned the Scammon farm for about seven years. In 1874, the couple moved to the San Bernardino region of California. There, James served as an itinerant pastor covering churches in Los Angeles, Riverside, Colton and San Bernardino. In 1878, for health reasons, he moved to Oakland, where he became the minister at the Second Presbyterian Church of Oakland.

In early January 1882, James had foot surgery. The doctor prescribed two medicines, an oral tonic and an external wash of carbolic acid. On January 5, his wife accidentally poisoned him by giving him carbolic acid, thinking it was the oral tonic. He died within minutes.

Very few of his paintings survive, and it is not known if he painted any of Moosehead Lake while residing here, but with the view, it is hard to believe he didn't.

Left: Reverend James Cameron served as the minister of the Union Church of Greenville from 1869 until June 30, 1871. Before coming to Greenville, he gained fame as a portrait and landscape painter. *Collection of the Moosehead Historical Society, accession number 1996.07.07.*

Right: Emma Cameron, shown here, and her husband, James, purchased the Scammon farm in 1865. *Collection of the Moosehead Historical Society, accession number 2010.15.0026.*

The Camerons sold the Greenville property to Victor W. Macfarlane for $5,400 on July 3, 1872. Macfarlane took out a mortgage on the land from the Camerons for $4,400 and, in 1879, built his summer cottage up the road from the original farmhouse. This will be discussed further in the next chapter.

In 1909, Macfarlane was running ads in an attempt to rent out the farm, and in 1913, he put the entire property up for sale. The July 1, 1909 issue of the *Piscataquis Observer* mentions that Mr. and Mrs. W.E. Atwood of New Britain, Connecticut, were leasing Macfarlane's house. The April 24, 1913 issue reports that W.S. Whitney, who had been living on the Macfarlane farm, had moved his family to South Orrington.

The property was eventually purchased by Andrew Jackson Sloper and his sons, Harold and William, on August 25, 1915. Andrew built a new home known as Greenslope between the existing farmhouse and the summer house Macfarlane had built. Harold used the Macfarlane House and rented out the farmhouse. William Sloper did not seem to have an official residence there and most likely stayed with one of the other two when he visited. The farmhouse was rented almost the entire time the Slopers owned it. It was at first occupied by Bert Hoskins and his wife, who was Harold and William Sloper's cousin. The family moved to Southern Pines, North Carolina, in September 1921. At that time, Clara Johnston and her family moved in, staying in the farmhouse for thirty years.

Carl A. and Edith S. Tornquist purchased the eight-acre lot that contained the farmhouse on June 7, 1947. The deed for the farmhouse property also shows the Tornquists purchased "the Shore" lot, located near the end of Shoals road, and the "Spring Lot," described as the supplier of water to the farm and buildings included in it. The Spring Lot description states that a pipeline runs from the spring down to the existing buildings. So, the spring was in use as a water source for the farm and buildings until at least 1947.

A 1948 article about the new Horizons West development mentions the houses that were being built along Lily Bay Road. We know the farmhouse was still standing in 1948 because the article notes that Ralph Anderson was already established opposite its "now rapidly dwindling remains."

The farmhouse was removed sometime between 1948 and 1953. In 1953–54, the Tornquists built the house that is currently there, close to the same location as the original. The Tornquists moved to Greenville in 1946 after Carl sold his interest in Mason & Parker Manufacturing in Winchendon,

After the original Scammon farmhouse was removed in the early 1950s, Carl and Edith Tornquist built a Cape Cod–style home on the same location. This photo shows it being built in 1954. *Courtesy Prudy Tornquist Richards.*

Massachusetts, where he had been the president. He became president of Eastern Pine Sales in Greenville, operating a lumber company and sawmill where Ware-Butler Building Supply is currently located.

Tornquist also made furniture and built a large workshop on the location of the old Scammon barn to house his operation. He sold wooden items at a little store called the Little Pine House, which was located above his home on Lily Bay Road. According to his granddaughter Prudy Tornquist Richards, the store was unmanned and operated on the honor system. She also stated that the original store building was later moved to the current location of the Spotted Cat Winery in Greenville.

On November 21, 1966, the Tornquists sold the house and property to Herbert and Thelma M. Cochrane. The Tornquists continued to live in the house for a few years until the Cochranes retired and moved to Greenville full time. The Cochranes operated Allagash Canoe Trips out of that location and owned the property until their deaths in 2004. At that time, their son Warren H. Cochrane became the owner. Upon his death on February 23, 2019, his wife, Linda Koski, became the sole owner.

Chapter 2

THE FAMOUS MACFARLANE HOUSE

The Macfarlane House, also known as the Sloper House and the Yellow House, is probably the second most famous landmark in the area, after the Blair Hill Inn. It was the second house built on the original Scammon farm. For the purposes of this book, the building will be called the Macfarlane House because it was built by Victor Wells Macfarlane.

Macfarlane was a Civil War veteran, a prominent businessman and a Maine state legislator. He was born on August 27, 1844, in Yonkers, New York, to Duncan and Mary Ann Macfarlane, both natives of Scotland. It is important to note the correct spelling of his name is "Macfarlane," even though it appears incorrectly as "Macfarland" on many maps and postcards.

Census data for 1850 shows Victor at age six living in Yonkers with his parents, Duncan Macfarlane, age thirty-eight, a baker, and his wife, Mary, age thirty-seven. Also living in the household were Victor's sister, Mary, age fifteen, and four journeyman bakers. The 1860 census lists Victor as being a student at age sixteen. Less than two years later, he would be fighting in the Civil War.

Victor enlisted in the Seventh Regiment of the National Guard of New York, eventually rising to the rank of major in the Seventeenth Regiment. He enlisted three times, serving from May 25, 1862, to September 5, 1862; from September 9, 1862, to January 13, 1863; and from July 8, 1863, to August 13, 1863.

Victor married Zanina Nelson on May 24, 1865. Born on April 12, 1845, in Peekskill, New York, Zanina was the daughter of Thomas and Cornelia

Louisa Seymour Nelson. It is interesting to note that Zanina's father was a Supreme Court justice of the Territory of Oregon from 1851 to 1853, having been appointed by President Millard Fillmore.

After the war, Victor was in business in New York City. In 1883, he moved to Chicago to operate a grain business. He was also involved with the Chicago Board of Trade and remained in Chicago until 1890, when he moved to Greenville for health reasons. He already had summered in Greenville on 450 acres he owned that had formerly been lots 80, 81, 82, 85 and 86 of the Scammon farm. These lots included the original Scammon farmhouse and barns as well as his summer home, the Macfarlane House.

Victor W. Macfarlane, shown here, was originally from New York. He fought in the Civil War and eventually became a Maine state senator. *Collection of the Moosehead Historical Society.*

Victor's presence in Greenville had lasting effects on the area. His life in Chicago connected him to a number of other influential people who also ended up calling Greenville home. Macfarlane served on the Chicago Board of Trade with Lyman Blair Sr. and Arthur A. Crafts. Blair's son, of course, built what is now the Blair Hill Inn. Crafts, who came to Greenville in the late 1800s, operated a number of businesses, including a sporting goods store and the Squaw Mountain Inn. No doubt they all traveled in the same social circles.

When Victor purchased the Scammon farm in 1872, the 450 acres included both woods and farmland along with a house and barn. He built his first cottage at the location of the current Macfarlane House in 1879. Farrar's guidebook from 1879 states that, in the spring of 1879, a large house was erected at "the Macfarlane Place." It was said to be capable of accommodating fifteen to twenty people and would serve as a clubhouse for Mr. Macfarlane's friends. It isn't hard to imagine why he selected the site. The spot features incredible views of Moosehead Lake.

The Macfarlane Place was included in a number of travel guides in the late 1800s. These include the *Guide to Moosehead Lake, and Northern Maine, with Map* by John M. Way Jr., published in 1874; *Farrar's Illustrated Guidebook to Moosehead Lake*, published in 1879; and *Moosehead Lake and Vicinity*, published by S.S. Davis and S.J. Chase of Foxcroft, Maine, in 1891. The latter booklet contains a photo of the original Macfarlane House, which burned down

The original Macfarlane cottage shown here was built in 1870 and burned down in 1894. It was replaced with the current cottage. This photo, the only one known of the original cottage, was published in a booklet titled *Moosehead Lake and Vicinity* printed in 1891 by S.S. Davis and S.J. Chase of Foxcroft, Maine. *Collection of the Moosehead Historical Society, accession number 1998.22.04A.*

in 1894. The *Portland Transcript*, published on May 13, 1896, mentions that Macfarlane had decided to rebuild the summer home that burned two summers previously. The rebuilt house is the one that still exists today. On August 22, 1896, Victor sold an eight-acre tract of land to Andrew Jackson Sloper of New Britain, Connecticut, perhaps to fund the rebuilding of his summer house.

Victor was active in the community and in local business. In 1891, he established the Greenville Manufacturing Company, a veneer mill located on the shore of Moosehead Lake. The *Piscataquis Observer* ran an article on September 29, 1892, explaining the entire veneer mill process. It states the mill included three buildings, an engine house, a main mill and a drying and storage room. It also says the doors bore the words "No Admittance" but people were free to enter as long as they didn't interfere with the workmen or machinery. The article doesn't specify which of the building's doors bear the words, but it's presumed that it refers to the doors on the main mill.

The *Piscataquis Observer* reported in the June 29, 1899 edition that V.W. Macfarlane had a crew of men tearing down the veneer mill in Shirley the previous week and that the mill would be relocated to Greenville. After the move, the plant was destroyed by fire and rebuilt in 1904. In October

1905, Victor formed the Veneer Box and Panel Company. In June 1906, he transferred the mill property over to the company, and as company president, he signed a lease with the H.M. Shaw Manufacturing Company to rent 6.7 acres around the mill site. The mill property itself was only about a half acre in size.

In 1899, Macfarlane was elected to the Maine state legislature, and in 1901, he was elected state senator from Piscataquis County. An article from the *Lewiston Journal* in 1901 states that Senator Macfarlane was the driving force behind the building of the fish hatchery at Moosehead Lake, having successfully secured $5,000 in funding for it.

Census data for 1900 shows Victor living in Greenville and lists his occupation as both manufacturer and farmer. His household also included his wife, Zanina; a maid named Kate Hibbard; a cook named Lizzie Rantal; a chore boy named George Steward; and three summer boarders, Lloyd Johnson, William Johnson and Ann Johnson.

Victor was also a leader in the Kineo Street Railway Company, which proposed a standard-gauge railroad three miles from Squaw Mountain Township to the town of Greenville, according to the March 27, 1902 issue of the *Piscataquis Observer*. Construction was to start in the spring once the frost was out of the ground, though it appears it was never built. The capital stock in the company was $25,000. In addition to Macfarlane, directors of the company were Allen Quimby of Greenville and Frank E. Guernsey of Dover. Other stockholders were Arthur E. Baxter and Warren H. Trafton, both of Greenville. At that time, the railway firm was the most northerly company in Maine to file articles of association.

In July 1907, the Veneer Box and Panel Company took a mortgage out with the Knickerbocker Trust Co. in New York. A month later, the company's board of directors moved the headquarters from Greenville to Portland, Maine. By October 28, 1907, the company was bankrupt. Fredrick Hale was appointed trustee for the bankrupt company and was asked to sell the assets. On February 25, 1908, the company was sold at public auction to Charles Taylor Hall, who was the high bidder at $25,000. The property was transferred into Charles's name on April 27, 1908, ending Victor Macfarlane's involvement with the mill. Hall founded the Veneer Products Company on December 5, 1908, and this property eventually would become Atlas Plywood Corporation.

Victor and Zanina had one daughter, Cornelia Seymour Macfarlane, who married Lyman Blair Jr. on July 19, 1886. Zanina died suddenly at their house in Greenville on April 20, 1903. The 1910 census for Greenville

This photo postcard shows the view looking down from the hill on Lyman Blair's property to Moosehead Lake, where the Macfarlane House and garage were located. *Authors' collection.*

shows Victor living with Lyman and Cornelia. On October 30, 1913, Victor married his second wife, Blanche Elizabeth Bailey.

In 1909, Victor advertised that the farmhouse and one hundred acres of his property were available for rent. The ad stated the eight-room farmhouse had running water and an attached stable, along with a larger barn that could house seventy-five cows. The barn also had running water, and farm machinery would be included in the rental.

Macfarlane ran an ad in September 1913 listing his farm for sale. The ad, a clipping of which is in the Moosehead Historical Society collection without the name of the publication, says the farm consisted of four hundred acres, with one hundred acres in cultivation and the rest in forest growth. Macfarlane's address was listed as 235 Fifth Avenue, New York, NY.

The September 8, 1915 issue of the *Hartford Courant* contains an article announcing that Andrew J. Sloper and his two sons, Harold T. and William T., had purchased the Macfarlane House and four-hundred-acre farm. The transfer, which included lots 80, 81, 82, 85, 86 and 87 of the original Stanton survey, took place on August 25, 1915, according to deeds filed in the courthouse. Each of the three buyers took out a $5,000 mortgage.

Victor died on October 15, 1917.

Andrew Sloper built a new home on the property, calling it Greenslope. His son Harold summered in the original Macfarlane House.

This view from the Lyman Blair property looking at the Macfarlane House and garage, with Moosehead Lake in the background, dates to when Harold Sloper owned the house. *Copy from the original negative, authors' collection, now in the Moosehead Historical Society Collection.*

Sloper's other son, William, kept a low profile. He had survived the sinking of the *Titanic* and then spent the rest of his life defending himself for it.

When the *Titanic* was about to set sail on its maiden voyage, William was twenty-eight and scheduled to return from England aboard the *Mauretania*. However, he ran into a friend, Alice Fortune, who had sailed to England with her family on the same ship as William. She told him about twenty other people from the first ship were passengers on the *Titanic*. He promised her he would stop by the Cunard Lines office and see if he could get a refund for his trip on the *Mauretania* and sail on the *Titanic* instead. As fate would have it, he was able to do so.

Once aboard the *Titanic*, he met Dorothy Gibson, who was a prominent actress at that time. She and her mother asked William if he would join them playing bridge. At 11:30 p.m. on April 14, 1912, they were still playing and were asked to retire so the steward could turn out the lights. Shortly after retiring, the ship hit the iceberg, and the group was reunited on the starboard side of the ship.

After William and others put on their life preservers, the ship's crew began loading the first lifeboat, number 7. An officer announced that any passenger could board the lifeboat. Most people did not believe the *Titanic* would sink, so few were interested in getting off the ship. William helped Dorothy and her mother into the lifeboat, and then Dorothy became hysterical, grabbed

William's hand and insisted he board. He was allowed to board because crews on the starboard side were loading women and children first but not necessarily excluding men. The boat in question was less than half full, so no one had an issue with him or other male passengers boarding. On the port side of the ship, however, crews were loading only women and children into lifeboats. Men were excluded.

After floating for most of the night in the tiny lifeboats in the icy cold waters, William and other survivors were rescued and taken to New York. William's father and brother met him there. While they were eating, a reporter tried to get an interview with William. However, Andrew and Harold "strong armed" the reporter in an attempt to thwart his efforts to get a story from William, who wanted to give his story instead to his local paper in Connecticut. The next day, an article appeared in the New York paper accusing William of dressing like a woman to get on the lifeboat. Andrew convinced William not to sue the paper, thinking it would blow over and be forgotten. But William spent the rest of his life defending himself from that lie.

A few months after the sinking of the *Titanic*, Andrew and Harold bought out William's portion of the Scammon farm. The transfer was reported in the September 20, 1917 edition of the *Piscataquis Observer*.

Upon Andrew's death on June 2, 1933, Harold Sloper and his wife, Carlotta C. Sloper, became the primary owners of the Macfarlane House and summered there for many years with their three children, Carlotta, Emily and Ella. Harold died on March 2, 1945, making Carlotta the sole owner.

On September 23, 1946, Carlotta; Andrew's widow, Myra; and Andrew and Myra's son, Erwin, entered into an agreement to clarify ownership of all the properties that had been purchased together by Andrew, Harold and William.

Carlotta's portion was defined as lot 87; a parcel in lot 80; the barn/garage and land fifty feet around it; the Harold T. Sloper summer residence, aka the Macfarlane House; and water rights to the residence. She also had control of the sap house on lots 85 or 86 with the right to remove it anytime within three years unless Erwin bought it. The sap house is believed to have been located on Sap House Road off Shoals Road, but its exact location is unknown. No records showing its location are known to exist.

Erwin's portion was lot 85 except for the Blair or Hoops Lot or Point and the right-of-way to it. His portion also included lot 86 except for the Nicholas lots and Myra W. Sloper lots and buildings on the shore of Moosehead, lot 81 together with buildings on it and lot 82. Along with the property transfers,

Carlotta Sloper, daughter of Harold and Carlotta Sloper, owned the Macfarlane House when this photo was taken in 1960. Edmund Bigney recalled Carlotta as being down to earth and friendly and that she drove a Willys Jeep station wagon. *Collection of the Moosehead Historical Society, accession number 2011.106.0001.*

Carlotta agreed to give a quitclaim deed lifting all building restrictions on Myra's land and homestead, Greenslope. Erwin also paid Carlotta $4,000 in cash when the deeds were exchanged.

In a deed dated October 1, 1948, Carlotta transferred the property known as the Blair or Hoops Lot or Point along with the right-of-way to Erwin.

Carlotta owned the Macfarlane House until August 15, 1955, when it was transferred to her daughter, Carlotta Sloper. The transaction was recorded in the county deed book volume 309, page 409. The elder Carlotta died on December 25, 1955. The younger Carlotta owned the house until November 6, 1984, when it was sold to Lutz N. and Waltraud A. Wallem, as shown in deed book 572, page 43. The younger Carlotta died on October 14, 1985.

Over the next several years, the Macfarlane House bounced from owner to owner, and various pieces of land were subdivided off and developed. The Wallems owned the Macfarlane House until January 8, 1987, when it was transferred to the Devlin Corp. The main property around the Macfarlane House was divided into three lots. The Wallems kept a lot to the north on Lily Bay Road and lot 3, as well as four lots on the shore along Sloper Road in a new development called Moosehead Lake Properties that Devlin Corp. had created in 1986. The Devlin Corp. transferred lot 2 containing the Macfarlane House to John M. Goodwin on January 19, 1988. The Devlin Corp. transferred lot 1 to K.O.A. Inc. on January 19, 1988, and on February 5, 1988, John M. Goodwin transferred lot 2, containing the Macfarlane House, to K.O.A. Inc., which transferred the property and house to George R. Gould Jr. and Deborah Johnson on December 30, 1988. On August 2, 1991, Gould and Johnson transferred it to George R. Gould Sr.

George R. Gould Sr. transferred it to Lisette Fauteux on January 4, 1993, and she owned it until December 21, 2017, when she sold it to the current owner, Stephen Foster. Since then, he and his wife, Suzanne, have been working to restore and renovate the house, totally rebuilding it from the inside out on a new foundation. While digging, they found charred remains of the original house that had burned.

Chapter 3

THE BLAIR MANSION

Lily Bay Road leaves the village of Greenville, going about two miles mostly uphill to reveal a spectacular mansion on the right-hand side. Its location high above the Macfarlane House provides an amazing view of the lake. This is, of course, the Blair Hill Inn, which opened in the late 1990s under the ownership of Daniel and Ruth McLaughlin. The current owner, Jennifer Whitlow, now operates it year round with expanded dining.

While the Blair Hill Inn serves as a familiar landmark to residents and visitors alike, it was not always an inn. In fact, it was built between 1889 and 1891 as a private residence, and it served as a private residence for nearly one hundred years.

The area in which the inn is located is called Blair Hill because of Lyman Blair Jr., a wealthy businessman who raised farm animals and built lavish gardens to serve as the backdrop for summer parties. An April 11, 1901 article in the *Chicago Inter Ocean* newspaper states that Blair was in Chicago "stealthily laying plans, so I hear, for the summer diversion." The piece went on to say that his summer home in Greenville could hold twenty-five guests, and rarely a week went by in the dog days of summer that it was not full. "Last year for example, the Blairs had so many happy outsiders with them that it was found necessary to purchase three new cows in order to provide extra cream, not to speak of the milk punches," the articles states, adding that Blair's income was so large that "it takes a man of the widest resource to spend it intelligently."

Lyman Blair Jr. was born on April 28, 1864, in Chicago, the son of Lyman Sr. and Mary Francis (De Groff) Blair. Lyman Jr. had two sisters: Emma, who

This photo of Lyman Blair from July 1933 shows him dressed in his finest clothing. *Collection of the Moosehead Historical Society, accession number 2000.0017.*

married Cyrus Hall Adams, and Mary, who married Chauncey Keep. Both men were from wealthy Chicago families.

Lyman Sr. had built a fortune with his brother, Chauncey, in the grain business in Michigan City, Illinois. Their firm was at first called C.B. & L. Blair, but they later changed the name to Blair & Blair. Chauncey eventually moved to Chicago, where he became the president of the Bank of the State of Indiana. Lyman Sr. soon followed, relocating to Chicago, where he continued to operate the Blair & Blair grain business. He got involved with the Chicago Board of Trade and played a role in forming the Chicago Stock Exchange in 1865.

On September 25, 1883, when Lyman Sr. was at the Tolleston Club outside Chicago, his gun discharged accidentally, killing him. Rumors circulated that his death was a suicide, causing grain and pork prices to fall for a short time. Letters were published in newspapers by other members of the Tolleston Club describing the accident in an effort to assure the public that the death was indeed an accident.

So, at the age of nineteen, Lyman Jr. found himself without a father. Lyman Sr. left his son only a small portion of his estate, estimated to be worth $750,000. According to the *Chicago Inter Ocean*, which ran an excerpt of the will, Lyman Sr. left the homestead and household goods to his wife and gave $1,000 to each of two nieces, Carrie Densmore and Linda Harris. The remainder of the estate was split four ways. His wife and two daughters each received a quarter. The last quarter went to his wife and Lyman together as "spending money" with the stipulation that Lyman Jr.'s share would go to the family if he were to marry. Lyman Jr. would also receive a quarter of the trust fund, not to exceed $25,000, if, at the age of twenty-five, he was engaged in business.

The reason Lyman Sr. specifically stipulated that Lyman Jr. could not get married without losing his inheritance is not known, but apparently, it didn't deter the younger Blair, who married Cornelia Macfarlane on July 19, 1886, when he was twenty-two.

Cornelia was the daughter of Victor and Zanina (Nelson) Macfarlane. As discussed in the previous chapter, Victor was originally from New York State, having served in the Civil War until 1863. After the war, he was in business in New York City until 1883, when he moved to Chicago to operate a grain business. Like Lyman Blair Sr., Macfarlane was involved with the Chicago Board of Trade. He had summered in Greenville since 1872 on his property, the original Edmund Scammon farm.

Before moving to Greenville, Lyman Jr. spent four years working for Merchants National Bank and then taking a position at Watson, Little and Company, a retail coal firm. He remained employed there until March 1889, when he started his own coal business, Lyman Blair and Co., which he ran until May 1891. At that time, he moved to Greenville and became the vice president and treasurer of the Greenville Manufacturing Company.

Lyman Jr. and Cornelia started building their house, which would eventually become the Blair Hill Inn, in 1889. The house, which took two years to build, overlooked Cornelia's parents' house. The Blairs moved in on December 23, 1891. The house would boast ten bedrooms and four baths and overlook Moosehead Lake with one of the best views.

This photo postcard shows the Blair Mansion from Lily Bay Road. The farm buildings and greenhouses can be seen on the right. *Authors' collection.*

This photo postcard shows the Blair Mansion from the Macfarlane property. The car to the right is parked along Lily Bay Road, and the occupants are getting water from a spring along the road. *Authors' collection.*

The land on which the house was located had been transferred from Zanina Macfarlane to her daughter, Cornelia Blair, on September 29, 1892, as shown in the county deed book volume 112, page 314. On April 2, 1907, Victor Macfarlane transferred another lot on Moosehead Lake to Cornelia. That lot, located on the south shore of Sandy Bay, is still referred to in deeds as the "Blair or Hoops Lot or Point." Thomas Hoops was the next owner of that property, having purchased it from Lyman Jr. on July 2, 1924, after Cornelia's death. Hoops sold it to Harold Sloper in 1935.

The Blairs were active in the community. Cornelia was involved with the local Union Church and was instrumental in getting the memorial tablet dedicated to Greenville soldiers built. In 1917, she organized the Moosehead Lake Chapter of the Women's Naval Service League Inc., where she served as the regent. Lyman was a member of the Masons and the Columbia Lodge in Greenville and the Anah Temple in Bangor.

Sometime after moving to Greenville, Lyman became interested in farming, naming his estate Hillside Farms. He built multiple barns and greenhouses and raised registered Guernsey cattle, Chester White swine, Scotch collie dogs, Rhode Island Red and White Wyandotte poultry and Oxford Down sheep.

In December 1904, Blair took up active management of his stock farm and became an agriculturist and breeder. The February 27, 1904 edition of the *New England Farmer* out of Boston ran a letter from Blair that reported his manager was in New York buying a Guernsey heifer at a staggering price and afterward was headed to New Jersey to visit another herd. Blair's letter says his young stock of sheep was selling fast and he was booking orders for animals before they were born. An interesting and rather forward-thinking statement for the time was included in the letter: "If it was not for the trouble in getting good, careful farm labor, that is, men that would take interest in their work and treat the animals gently, I would add many more breeding animals in every department. One thing I insist upon above all others: every animal should be treated with kindness and not abuse."

Lyman eventually expanded to include another farm he called the Annex. It does not appear that he purchased this farm but rather leased or rented it. The Annex was the former Edmund M. Sawyer farm located off Scammon Road on what is now Higgins Road. When the owners, Fred and Florence Pygensky, were selling this property in 1942, the deed stated that lot 77 was formerly known as the Edmund M. Sawyer place and that lot 77 "has been known for many years as 'The Annex' and is the same premises as formerly

The sign for Hillside Gardens was located at the end of the Blair mansion driveway on Lily Bay Road, as seen in this photo postcard. The welcome sign to the left also says "Hillside Gardens" with a Masons logo on it. Lyman Blair was a Mason and often used the Mason logo in the flower garden designs. *Authors' collection.*

occupied by Lyman Blair as an annex to the Hillside Farm." The Annex was most likely accessed directly from Blair's Hillside Farm through the woods on the old road that originally ended at the Scammon farm. It is discussed in chapter 1.

The January 17, 1907 issue of *Maine Farmer* includes an article about the Moosehead Lake Sanatorium that says twenty Ohio Improved Chester White swine were kept at the hospital and these were registered stock from Hillside Farms.

In a February 5, 1907 letter to the Greenville selectmen, Blair asked to be reimbursed for maintaining two water troughs. One of them was located near the Annex and ran in the summer, and the other was situated between his house and the Macfarlane House on the road. This one had water in it year round, and it was used by the public when traveling on the roadway. Bills from 1906 also show Blair assessed Greenville three dollars each to maintain the troughs in 1904 and 1905.

The November 21, 1914 issue of the *Bangor Daily News* includes an article titled "Fine Cows at Hillside Farm" that says Lyman was a leading exhibitor at different state and county fairs, winning many blue ribbons with his Guernsey cows. Seven of his cows were being tested by the University of Maine for the amount of milk and milk fat they produced. The December 12, 1914 issue of the same paper reports Blair was at the state dairy conference and that he was going to experiment in raising mule foot hogs on his farm. He was already raising Chester White pigs, and he ran an ad in the August 26, 1915 edition for six- to eight-week-old Chester White boars and sows that he was selling for five dollars each.

It is unclear how much capacity Hillside Farms had for milk production or if the main goal was animal husbandry and breeding. Two milk bottles from Hillside Farms are known to exist. They are glass quart bottles with "Hillside Farms Greenville Maine" embossed on them. They also carry the Maine seal on the bottoms. It is unknown whether these bottles were for his own use on his estate or whether he bottled and sold milk to others. Most people in Greenville remember Indian Hill Farms being the main source for milk in Greenville. However, Hillside Farms may predate the later success of Indian Hill, and they may have sold milk, as indicated by the milk bottles.

Blair didn't operate the farm on his own. The 1910 census shows Lyman, Cornelia, Victor Macfarlane, a boarder, three hired men and eight servants living at Hillside. The 1920 census shows Lyman, Cornelia, an employee and two servants.

An April 9, 1917 accounting of his farm animals from the Moosehead Historical Society archives shows Blair had one boar, four sows, three young sows, two small pigs, four horses, seven cows, four heifers, three bulls and three "scrub" cows. Scrub cows are a breed originally from Florida that were descendants of stray cows left behind by the Spanish. They were smaller and bonier and once described as "4H; hide, hair, hoofs and horns."

Cornelia died on December 25, 1923, after having been dangerously ill for several weeks, according to a January 3, 1924 report in the *Piscataquis Observer*. The article states she was one of the "Home Guard" during the World War and that "she gave her life in the cause of freedom, just as truly as did any of our soldiers who gave theirs on the battlefield, as her constant work in the Navy League and other helpful agencies planted the germs of disease which finally brought an end to a busy, helpful life."

The 1930 census shows Lyman, three lodgers and one servant living on the estate. The lodgers included Frederick Bigney; his wife, Mildred; and their four-year-old son, Frederick. The elder Frederick Bigney was the farm superintendent, and Mildred was Lyman's secretary and housekeeper. The 1940 census shows the Bigneys still living there along with a cook, a maid and a laborer.

Between 1892 and 1915, Blair took ownership of portions of town lots 79, 80 and 88 that were located east of Main Street, now Lily Bay Road.

This photo postcard shows the Blair Mansion and gardens looking from the south. *Authors' collection*.

This postcard illustration shows Hillside Gardens from the south side of the mansion. Moosehead Lake is in the background. *Authors' collection.*

The portion of lot 80 came from the Macfarlanes. Lot 79 and a portion of lot 88 were purchased from E. Adeline Bigney, William L. Rogers and Anna W. Varney. Blair transferred a piece of land to Norman Cooley in 1930, according to deed book volume 236, page 282. Cooley was a friend of his, and the unofficial word is that the land was transferred to Cooley because of a gambling debt. See chapter 4.

By the mid-1930s, Lyman began calling his Hillside Farm "Hillside Gardens." The gardens became a tourist attraction to some extent, and people drove to tour his gardens. An article from the *Bangor Daily News* of November 19, 1935, states that people would be interested to know that "the *News* received several pansies from Mr. Blair Monday, picked in his garden Sunday." So, 1935 must have been a warm year for Lyman to still have pansies in November, or he may have grown them in a greenhouse. The *Bangor Daily News* reported on July 3, 1937, that Mr. Stetson, a well-known Bangor lumberman, and his wife traveled up to the Moosehead Coffee House and then went to see Lyman Blair's rock garden.

The Blairs had no children. Lyman died on September 12, 1946, and his home was left to his nephew, Cyrus Adams Jr., a senior partner of the law firm of Isham, Lincoln & Beale. The firm was founded by Robert Todd Lincoln, son of President Abraham Lincoln, and two associates. Cyrus used the home only in the summer. He later transferred more land to Cooley in 1946, as shown in county deed book volume 285, page 30.

On July 22, 1960, Cyrus sold the estate to Leroy and Bernice Edwards, as shown in county deed book volume 336, page 352. The Edwardses used the home primarily as a summer residence. Leroy Edwards died in 1973, and in 1977, Bernice transferred 37.6 acres in town lots 79 and 88 to Carl Zuendel. In 1978, she transferred 32.33 acres of town lot 79 to James Hilton. Bernice and her son, Brad Edwards, ran the property as Hillside Gardens Bed and Breakfast for a period. A brochure, currently in the archives of the Moosehead Historical Society, states the property contained seventy-eight acres to explore. It was listed for sale for a number of years. A June 1985 ad in *Yankee Homes* showed an asking price of $495,000. Bernice Edwards owned the property until July 30, 1990, when she sold it to Kenneth and Mary Hughes, as per county deed book volume 778, page 340. Kenneth and Mary were the founders and owners of the still popular restaurant Kelly's Landing, located on Moosehead Lake in Greenville Junction.

Mary Hughes and her daughter, Marty, operated the property as Hillside Gardens Bed and Breakfast. The Hugheses sold the property to Ellen L. Jobin on October 7, 1994, as per county deed book volume 959, page 61. She used the house as a private residence until November 25, 1997, when she sold it to the McLaughlins. They sold their family home in Chicago and moved into the Blair mansion, opening it seasonally as the Blair Hill Inn one month later. While running their new business, the McLaughlins, with the help of master carpenter Larry Lewis, began the process of rewiring and replumbing and restoring the kitchen, guest rooms and bathrooms.

The McLaughlins sold the Blair Hill Inn and property to Blair Hill Inn LLC, Jennifer Whitlow, on April 15, 2022, and she continues to operate it as the Blair Hill Inn.

Chapter 4

THE COOLEY HOUSE

Most people don't know about the Cooley house on Blair Hill because it can't be seen from Lily Bay Road. It's hidden in the woods, up the driveway past the Blair Hill Inn when heading north.

Although the name Cooley doesn't have the same familiar sound as Blair and Sloper, Norman Cooley had many local connections and summered here for many years. Lyman Blair Jr. transferred the rectangular 5.7-acre lot to him on October 29, 1930. According to the McLaughlins, Blair gave the property to Cooley to pay off a gambling debt. Cyrus Adams transferred an additional 13.7 acres to Cooley on November 9, 1946. This land adjoins the original lot and runs down the hill to Lily Bay Road.

An interesting provision in the original deed gave Cooley the "right to take water, in sufficient quantity to supply the premises hereby conveyed for domestic purposes, from said Blair's 16,000 gallon wood tank, situated near the artesian well at what is called the 'Old Windmill Tower' with the right to enter upon the adjoining land of said Blair to lay, relay and properly maintain all necessary pipes."

Cooley was born in August 1869. Census data for 1870 shows him at nine months old living in New Britain, Connecticut, with his father, George P., age forty; mother, Lucy, age twenty-nine; and a three-year-old brother, George, as well as a nurse, Lucy Graham, and a domestic servant, Kate Egan. His father was listed as a physician. The 1880 census shows the young Norman living with father, mother, brother, a coachman and a servant.

Mr. Norman P. Cooley

Opposite, top: This image of the Cooley house shows what it looked in 1936. It can also be seen on page 31 of the book *The History of Greenville 1836–1936*, by Emma True. *Collection of the Moosehead Historical Society, accession number 2021.0016.*

Opposite, bottom: The Cooley house appears to be closed up for the winter in this 1927 view of the Cooley Estate. Cooley stayed at the house only during the summer. *Collection of the Moosehead Historical Society, accession number 2001.29.0055.*

Above: This photo shows Lyman Blair on the left and Norman Cooley on the right. The unidentified woman in the middle could be May Butterworth. *Collection of the Moosehead Historical Society, accession number 2015.0314.*

Around 1894, Cooley married his wife, Mary, who was born in February 1869. Her maiden name is unknown. The 1900 census shows Norman and Mary S. living in the same household, and Cooley's occupation is listed as "capitalist."

In 1901, Cooley and Howard Stanley Hart started the Hart & Cooley Manufacturing Company. Hart had invented the steel heating register, which was superior to the cast-iron registers of the time. Hart & Cooley became the first company in the United States to make steel stamped warm air registers. The company was a success, and in the 1920s, the partners

In this photo of a get-together are, *from left,* Carlotta Sloper, Harold Sloper, May Butterworth, Norman Cooley, Cornelia Blair and Lyman Blair. The man sitting in the front is unidentified. *Collection of the Moosehead Historical Society, accession number 2015.0315.*

opened a manufacturing plant in Michigan. The Hart & Cooley Company is still in business today in Michigan.

Census data for 1930 lists Cooley's occupation as the president of a machine factory. His wife, Mary, is listed as living in the same household in New Britain, Connecticut, but she died sometime during the next decade because the 1940 census lists Norman as a widower.

The 1950 census shows that Cooley's household included a registered nurse, May Butterworth, living there as a lodger. A cook also lived with them at that time. Cooley often traveled to Bermuda with Butterworth and, at times, with his business partner, Howard Hart.

Upon Cooley's death on December 9, 1952, May F. Butterworth inherited the Cooley House. She was born in 1900 and lived in Cromwell, Connecticut. On February 28, 1984, she transferred ownership to herself and her sister Ruth P. Ecker. When Butterworth died on August 14, 1990, Ecker became the sole owner. Butterworth's obituary was very short, mentioning only that she spent her entire life in Cromwell and sixty summers on Blair Hill in Greenville.

On August 22, 1991, Ecker transferred ownership to herself and Cheryl E. Hohman, Julia Hohman and Todd W. Hohman. Ecker died on May 31, 2005, when ownership went to the Hohmans. On September 2, 2006, the Hohmans sold the property to Debbie B. Stankauskas. On March 14, 2019, Stankaukas sold it to the current owner, Sheehan Gallagher.

Chapter 5

GREENSLOPE

The Lodge at Moosehead Lake wasn't always a high-end lodging and dining facility. It started out as a summer home for Connecticut banker and businessman Andrew Jackson Sloper after he and his two sons, Harold T. and William T., purchased the Macfarlane farm in 1915.

Andrew Sloper was born on July 14, 1849, in Southampton, Connecticut, to Lambert and Emma Sloper. Lambert is listed as a farmer in the 1850 census. Before Andrew was ten years old, his family had moved to New Britain, Connecticut. He went to school there and graduated high school when he was fourteen. He spent one year at a normal school, which was the equivalent of college at the time.

Andrew went to work for a photographer and then at a dry goods store. In 1867, he became a messenger boy for the National Bank in New Britain. At the age of twenty, he was a bank teller, according to the 1870 census. He had become an assistant cashier by 1880, according to the census for that year. In 1895, he became president of the bank. The 1900 census indicates he was a bank official. In 1928, he was the chairman of the board of the bank. He was also a councilman and alderman in New Britain and was a state senator in 1901 and 1902.

Andrew married Ella Blackwell Thomson, who was born on June 13, 1853, in New Britain, Connecticut. She was the daughter of James and Angeline Thomson. Andrew and Ella had five children: Annie, Harold, an unnamed infant boy, William and Kenneth. Annie died before her first birthday. The unnamed infant probably died at birth. Ella died on August 25, 1910.

Above: Andrew Jackson Sloper and his second wife, Myra, standing on the front porch of Greenslope. *Collection of the Moosehead Historical Society, accession number 2003.21.0011.*

Opposite, top: Greenslope, shown here from the front, would eventually become the Lodge at Moosehead Lake. *Copy from the original negative, authors' collection, now in the Moosehead Historical Society Collection.*

Opposite, bottom: This photo, looking up at the west side of Greenslope from below and toward Moosehead Lake, probably dates to when Daniel F. and Helen J. Ancona owned it. *Collection of the Moosehead Historical Society, accession number 2017.60.0009.*

In 1911, Andrew married Myra J. Wilcox, who was born around 1882. She and Andrew had one son, Erwin Wilcox Sloper, on August 13, 1913. In 1917, Andrew built his house, Greenslope, near Lily Bay Road between the original Scammon farmhouse and the former Macfarlane House. Greenslope was used as a summer vacation home. Andrew transferred ownership of the house to Myra on August 13, 1917.

Andrew Jackson Sloper died on June 2, 1933. At the time of his death, he was the chairman of the board of the New Britain National Bank; president and treasurer of the New Britain Gas Light Company; a director of the American Hardware Corporation; a director of Landers, Frary & Clark; a director of North & Judd; a director of Union Manufacturing Company; a director of New Britain Machine Company; and a director of the Trumbull Electric Company.

After Andrew's death, his and Myra's son, Erwin, began running Greenslope as an inn with a restaurant. A July 2, 1936 ad in the *Piscataquis Observer* bragged that Greenslope, on Blair Hill, had excellent food. Luncheons were served from noon to 1:30 p.m., tea was served from 3:00 to 4:00 p.m. and dinner was available from 6:00 to 7:30 p.m. A 1937 ad says Greenslope was open for the season from July 1 to September 15 with a dining room and lounge.

Erwin married Anne Louise Baxter on July 30, 1939, in Greenville. On the marriage certificate, Erwin's occupation is listed as innkeeper. The August 3, 1939 wedding announcement published in the *Bangor Daily News* says Erwin is the proprietor of Greenslope.

In July 1947, Erwin started the Horizons West development on three hundred acres of the former MacFarlane farm. Myra retained ownership of Greenslope while Erwin concentrated on being a developer. Erwin and the Horizons West development are discussed in detail in chapter 6.

GREENSLOPE

On Blair's Hill

GREENVILLE, MAINE

EXCELLENT FOOD

Luncheon	12-1:30 E.S.T.
Tea	3-4 P.M., E.S.T.
Dinner	6-7:30 E.S.T.

Reservations for Card Parties Appreciated

Erwin Sloper ran Greenslope as an inn, as shown in this July 2, 1936 advertisement from the *Piscataquis Observer*. Greenslope was built by his father, Andrew Jackson Sloper, and remained under the ownership of his mother, Myra, at this time. *Authors' collection*.

On August 30, 1957, Myra transferred ownership of Greenslope to Daniel F. and Helen J. Ancona of Reading, Pennsylvania. The Anconas owned the property until Daniel died in March 1970. Helen transferred the property to Daniel S. and Eva B. Gurney of Costa Mesa, California, on November 13, 1970.

Daniel and Eva Gurney then transferred it to Lutz N. and Waltraud A. Wallem of Topsfield, Massachusetts, on March 15, 1978. The Wallems transferred the property to Ruth Cool and James Devlin of Greensville, Maine, on August 31, 1978.

Ruth and James turned Greenslope into the Lake View Manor, a restaurant and bed-and-breakfast that drew repeat customers from across the country, and then changed the name to the Devlin House Bed and Breakfast with the same result. Ruth and James sold the property to James D. Jr. and Jerry Horger Anderson of Greensville, Maine, on December 16, 1985.

The Andersons sold the property to Roger S. and Jennifer A. Cauchi of Stroudsburg, Pennsylvania, on March 11, 1991. The Cauchis turned it into the Lodge at Moosehead Lake and sold the property to Bruce and Sonda Hamilton of Greenville on June 22, 2001.

On May 30, 2007, the Hamiltons sold it to Lakeview Lodging Inc., Dennis D. and Linda J. Bortis. They sold it to the current owners, Highlands Lodging Inc., Lawrence P. Burgess and Beverley Burgess, on March 22, 2021. The Burgesses continue to operate it as the Lodge at Moosehead Lake.

Chapter 6

THE HORIZONS WEST DEVELOPMENT

As discussed in chapter 2, Carlotta Sloper, Myra Sloper and Erwin Sloper entered into an agreement to clarify ownership of their properties on September 23, 1946. This laid the groundwork for Horizons West, a development that encompassed much of the original Scammon/Macfarlane farm. The Horizons West subdivision opened up a lot of land on the east side of the lake to development that had previously been owned by one or two families. Many of the smaller homes seen along Lily Bay Road near the original Macfarlane House were part of this development.

Erwin and his wife started Horizons West in July 1947, though they had already begun selling lots in late 1946. Horizons West was said to be made up of about three hundred acres of the former Macfarlane farm. This was not its original name, however. An ad in the 1947 *Moosehead Lake Gateway to Happiness* booklet advertises it as a development called "End Ridge" with cottage lots and land on the eastern shore of Moosehead Lake and "home sites high above the lake on The Lily Bay Road." For an unknown reason, Anne and Erwin changed the name of their development, and their ad in the 1948 edition of the guide calls it "Horizons West (Formerly End Ridge)."

Four plans were drawn by E.J. and G.B. Smith. Plan 1, titled "House Lots Greenville, Maine, for Erwin W. Sloper," was drawn in February 1948. Plan 2, titled "Plan of House and Cottage Lots Greenville Maine for Erwin Sloper," was drawn in June 1948. Plans 3 and 4, titled "Cottage Lots Greenville, Maine, for Erwin W. Sloper," were drawn in June 1948 and

Horizons West was developed by Erwin and Anne Sloper along Lily Bay Road and Shoals Road. The ad is from the 1948 edition of the *Moosehead Lake Gateway to Happiness* booklet. *Authors' collection.*

October 1948, respectively. Lots in Plan 4 were designated by letter rather than by number. Lots were roughly one-half acre in size.

Plan 1 consisted of seventy-six lots on both sides of Lily Bay Road and down Shoals Road. This plan also proposed streets paralleling Lily Bay Road, one of which was four hundred feet below it and intersecting Shoals Road, while the other was four hundred feet above Lily Bay Road. Plan 2 consisted of thirty-one lots situated along proposed roads to be located off Shoals. Plan 3 consisted of twenty-six lots with sixteen along the lake and the others situated on proposed streets off Shoals. Plan 4 consisted of fifteen lots on the lake shore down what is now Big Hill Road and Horizons West Road.

Many cottages and permanent homes were built in the development in the 1940s and early 1950s. Because the lots were small, many people eventually bought more than one lot.

On the Horizons West Plan 1, Dr. Isaac Nelson and his wife, Amy, purchased lot 3 in 1947 and built a summer home. Nelson practiced medicine in New York for thirty-two years before moving to Greenville full time around 1960. He served as a doctor in Greenville until his death in 1976.

On lot 4, Ralph E. and Muriel L. Anderson built a house around 1948. According to the 1950 census, Ralph Anderson was the principal of the local junior high school, and Muriel was a nurse at the C.A. Dean Hospital. They owned the property until November 10, 1960, when they sold it to Glenys G. Pero, who sold it on December 27, 1979, to Carl G. and Dorothy M. Vogelman. The Vogelmans also operated Sunset Harbor Camps on Sand Bay, located a little farther down Lily Bay Road, from 1970 to 1993. They lived on the Horizons West property until May 18, 1995, when they sold it to Christian R. Picker. He sold it on December

23, 2004, to Dorinda S. Galbraith, and she sold it to the current owners, Dana A. and Amy R. Bishop, in 2006.

In 1948, T. Stephen Runcy bought lot 1 plus an adjacent smaller angular piece in Plan 1 and built a summer cottage, which is still in the Runcy family.

On September 6, 1947, Robert M. Diehl and his wife, V. Myrtle Diehl, purchased lots 9 and 10 and built a house there in 1952. Robert was a schoolteacher and later became principal of the high school. The couple sold the property on September 21, 1955, to Vaughn and Ruth Simpson. Vaughn worked at Atlas Plywood. Ruth died in 1968, and Vaughn retained ownership until June 17, 1970, when he sold it to Karl W. and Nancy E. Watler, who still own it.

Alban J. and Shirbie A. Pelletier purchased lots 6 and 7 on September 20, 1951. Alban also worked at Atlas Plywood. The Pelletiers sold the property to John and Edna Dyer on July 22, 1953. John Dyer grew up in Kokadjo, working as a guide and as a warden for the Maine Forestry Service before entering the military during World War II. After the war, he worked for Scott Paper and other lumber operations. Later, he became the office manager at Squaw Mountain and then worked at the C.A. Dean Hospital as a business manager and administrator.

The Dyers sold the property to Millard I. and Lillian M. Elsemore on June 6, 1956. Lillian's sister was Ruth Simpson, who, with her husband, Vaughn, had just purchased property across the street the year before. Both worked at Atlas Plywood, Millard as a foreman and Lillian as a dryer. In 1958, Millard became a widower. He sold the property to Clyde F. and Estelle M. Morton on August 21, 1967. Greenville tax records show that the Mortons built a house on the property between 1971 and 1974. The Mortons owned the property until October 21, 1993, when they sold it to Michael E. and Ellen L. Jobin. The house the Mortons built on the lot was removed around 1994, when the Jobins constructed the current house. The Jobins owned the property until July 20, 2006, when they sold it to Nancy Wescott. She sold the property to Sean and Johanna Billings on July 10, 2020.

As mentioned in chapter 1, Carl and Edith Tornquist built a home on the site of the original Scammon farmhouse along Lily Bay Road. The Tornquists also purchased lots 14, 16, 44, 45, 46 and 47 on Plan 1 from Erwin Sloper on January 15, 1951. Their son, John W. Tornquist, and his wife, Anne G., built a home there. John and Anne sold the property to Clarence A. and Ruth A. Lang on April 28, 1959. The Langs operated Sunset Harbor Camps on Sand Bay from 1950 to 1970, before the Vogelmans took over. The Lang family owned the house and the land until

This map from February 1948 shows Plan 1 of Erwin Sloper's Horizons West development. The road down the center is Lily Bay Road, and Shoals Road is on the bottom center. The roads that parallel Lily Bay Road are proposed roads that were never built. The proposed road to the right of the Spring Lot was moved to between lots 5 and 6 and also never built. Most of the lots were combined, and few houses were built on just one lot. *Courtesy Piscataquis County Courthouse.*

April 8, 1999, when it was sold to Roger E. and Carol G. Mills. Then, on June 29, 2001, the Millses sold it to Vikki L. and Charles K. Ryder. It was then sold to Grace M. Bardsley on May 26, 2005, and she sold it to Robert E. Tracy on July 1, 2021. The current owner, Jennifer M. Whitlow, purchased it on March 14, 2022.

Caroline Capen Teall purchased lots 27, 28 and 29 in Plan 1 on October 14, 1949, and built a cottage there. She owned it until her death in 1954. She left the property to her sister, Dorothy Bartlett, and brother, C. Norman Capen. The current owner, John Place, purchased it in 2000.

On September 6, 1950, as the Horizons West development was getting started, Myra Sloper sold a small piece of land across the road from Greenslope to George H. Thompson. He and his wife, Eleanor, would then go on to purchase the property behind them and to the north along Lily Bay Road until they owned more than forty acres.

Thompson owned the Thompson Candy Company in Meriden, Connecticut, a business started by George's grandfather, William H. Thompson, in 1879. Prudy Tornquist Richards, granddaughter of Carl and Edith Tornquist who lived across the street from the Thompsons, said that in the spring when the Thompsons came to their summer house, everyone wanted to visit because they brought candy from the factory.

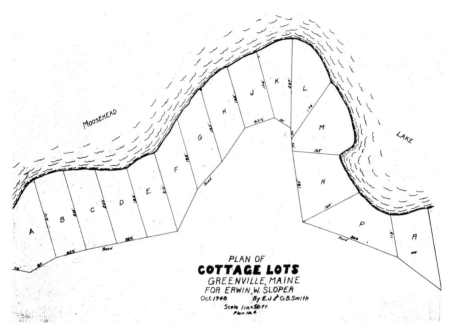

This map from October 1948 shows Plan 4 of Erwin Sloper's Horizons West. This location, which was known as the Blair or Hoops Point, was sold to Thomas Hoops on July 2, 1924. It had previously been deeded to Cornelia Blair by her father, Victor Macfarlane, on August 14, 1915. Courtesy *Piscataquis County Courthouse*.

The Thompsons built a ranch house on the property for use as a summer home. The Thompsons sold the property to James E. and Shelia McIver on August 14, 1980. After James's death in 2004, Shelia owned the property until October 24, 2014, when she sold it to the current owner, Anthony C. Loconte. He kept the original ranch house and built the additional buildings that make up the complex today.

During the approximately ten years that Erwin Sloper was active at Horizons West, he sold the majority of the lots in the four plans. In addition to the owners mentioned already, Erwin Sloper sold additional lots in Plan 1 as follows: lots 2 and 5 to Philip R. Keirstead; lots 8, 57 and 58 to Herbert I. McLane; lot 17 to John C. and Elizabeth B. Cass; lots 18, 19, 20 and 21 to Richard and Inda Chase; lots 22, 23 and 24 to Robert F. and Virginia A. Brattan; lot 25 to Mapel C. Kronholm; lots 30, 31, 32, 33, 34 and 35 to Llewellyn F. and Mary S. Wortman; and lots 36, 37, 49 and 50 to Helen C. and Emma R. Brogan.

Of the thirty-one lots in Plan 2, only two were sold by Erwin Sloper. They were lots 84 and 88, which were sold to Lawrence O. and Phyllis Rowe.

In Plan 3, which fronted Moosehead Lake, all the lots were sold by Erwin. Summer cottages were built on many of them. The lots and their owners were as follows: lots 1 and 2, Richard W. and Inga Chase; lots 3, 4, 5, 14, 15 and 16, Don and Marie Hubbard; lots 8, 9, 10 and 11, Robert H. and Rae G. Kahrs; lot 12, Oliver I. and Ivena E. Snow; and lot 13, Joseph E. and Frances McEachern.

In Plan 4, which also fronted Moosehead Lake, Erwin sold all but lot A. The other lot owners were as follows: lot B, Llewellyn F. and Mary S. Wortman; lots C, D and E, Carl and Pauline Spencer; lot F and G, Daniel F. and Helen J. Ancona; lots H and J, Pierre F. Ancona; lots K and L, Abe L. and Ida B. Goldsmith; lot M, Anne, Robert F. and Sally Anne Sloper; lot N, split among Pierre Ancona and Abe and Ida Goldsmith; and lots P and R, Richard and Igna Chase.

In this October 1958 aerial photo of Greenslope, Dr. Nelson's house and garage are visible in the upper left. Below Nelson's garage is Carl Tornquist's Little Pine House Furniture store. The store was located on Lily Bay Road in front of the Tornquist home, which would have been located to the right, outside the photo. *Collection of the Moosehead Historical Society.*

Erwin and Anne Sloper ended up getting divorced, and Anne moved to Texas with their two children. She sold lot M, which had belonged jointly to her and their children, to the Goldsmiths in 1956. Around 1957, Erwin moved to Phoenix, Arizona, and remarried. He was sending correspondence back to Maine as he finished up sales and needed to record deeds. On October 28, 1958, he sold all the land, subdivided or not, and his right, title and interest to any of the roads in the Horizons West development to Lawrence Rowe. Erwin died in Phoenix on March 2, 1960, at the young age of forty-six.

Lawrence Rowe continued selling the lots and property contained in Horizons West. One of the things that Rowe had to correct after purchasing the subdivision was an access point to Moosehead Lake for lots in the development not located on the water. In deeds for the properties Erwin had sold, he granted the lot owners the right to access Moosehead Lake but without specifying an access location. So, on March 14, 1966, Rowe dedicated lot 7 and the eastern portion of lot 6 as shown on Plan 3 as the access point for Horizons West property owners.

Rowe owned the development until January 14, 1971, when he sold the entire remaining property to James E. and Patricia M. Fitz-Patrick. The Fitz-Patricks subdivided the portion of the land that was located on the west side of Sap House Road into six lots, labeled AA through FF. In 1977, the property went into James Fitz-Patrick's name individually. He owned it until September 16, 1988, when he sold the development, including roads, to Wayne C. Shaw. Wayne and Virginia Shaw created a new subdivision on the lands west of Lily Bay Road along Shoals, Big Hill and Sap House Roads. The development, called Moosehead Heights, created much larger lots and, for the most part, ignored the smaller lot lines of the Horizons West subdivision. It also used the same lot for water access as the Horizons West development had done.

Chapter 7

THE MOOSEHEAD LODGE

The Moosehead Lodge was located on the lake at the end of what is now Shoals Road. At that time, the road was known as the Sloper-Corsa Road. Howard B. Corsa operated the lodge from 1945 to 1971.

Howard was the son of George H.B. and Grace Corsa. He was born on December 17, 1903, in Pound Ridge, New York. His family moved to Connecticut, and the 1910 census data shows Howard at age six living with his parents in Fairfield County, Connecticut. His father's occupation is listed as farmer.

Howard married Winifred Hopkins. In 1950, Howard was living in Wilton, Connecticut, with his wife and their four children, according to census data. Howard's occupation is listed as sporting lodge operator. He advertised the lodge in the Maine Publicity Bureau's *Maine Invites You* from the 1940s through the 1960s. The ads boasted fishing, hunting and sports, home cooking and reasonable rates.

Howard purchased the lodge from Roberta Johnson Nicholas on October 15, 1942. Although he purchased the property as one piece, Roberta and her father originally acquired it from Victor Macfarlane in four separate transactions. Roberta's father, Robert Wood Johnson I, purchased the first piece on October 29, 1906. He purchased adjoining property on September 23, 1908, and another tract on November 19, 1908. Roberta purchased the last of the four pieces on November 18, 1908. Robert died in 1910, and Roberta became the sole owner of all four pieces. To clearly define the borders of the property after the Slopers purchased all the surrounding property from Macfarlane, Roberta and Andrew and Harold Sloper transferred all

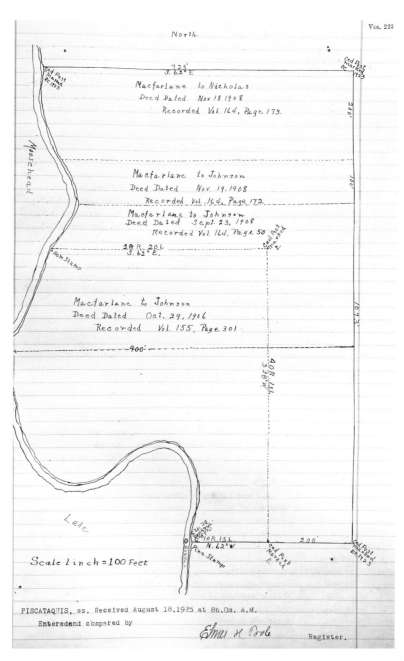

This plan drawn by Elmer B. Crowley shows the property owned by Roberta Johnson Nicholas as well as the individual lots purchased by her and her father, Robert Johnson. The plan was drawn up in 1925 to clarify the lot lines between Nicholas's property and the several members of the Sloper family. *Courtesy of the Piscataquis County Courthouse.*

the property back to the Slopers and had a plan drawn and new deeds issued back to Roberta for this purpose on August 12, 1925. These four parcels combined are what Roberta sold to Howard in 1942.

Roberta's father and his two brothers were the founding members of the Johnson & Johnson Company. Roberta's mother was Robert Wood Johnson's first wife, Ellen Cutler.

Roberta married Robert Carter Nicholas, and they lived in New Jersey. Her husband is listed as a broker living in Piscataway, New Jersey, in the 1930 census.

In the mid-1920s to 1930s, Roberta and her husband ran a fox farm on the Greenville site. Seward and Elizabeth Worster were the caretakers until late 1926. The November 11, 1926 issue of the *Piscataquis Observer* reports that the Worsters had given up their position as caretakers to Frank Jardine and that Frank had moved his family into the Nicholas cottage.

Frank was born in Kouchibouguac, Canada, and moved to Greenville around 1917. He married the Worsters' daughter, Clara, in 1919 and became a U.S. citizen seven years later. Three of his sisters also ended up living in Greenville.

The fox farm achieved a bit of notoriety from a May 12, 1927 article in the *Piscataquis Observer* titled "A Feline Foster Mother," about a mother cat at the Nicholas cottage and fox ranch. The cat, already the mother of three kittens, adopted two orphaned silver black foxes. The article went on to say that the mother cat was often somewhat confused when half her family meowed and the other half barked.

The 1930 census for Greenville shows the Jardine family still living at the cottage, with Frank's occupation listed as manager of a fox farm. It's unclear when the Nicholas fox farm shut down. The Great Depression ended most fox farming, and it was outlawed in Maine in 1952.

It's interesting to note that Roberta and her husband also operated a cattle ranch in Pima, Arizona, which is near Tucson. The 1940 census lists Robert and Roberta as operator and assistant operator, respectively.

Robert died on August 31, 1941, precipitating the sale of the property to Howard. In addition to purchasing the land from Roberta, Howard bought a tract abutting the original property from Erwin Sloper on November 25, 1946. That land included buildings, piers and wharves. On February 20, 1951, he purchased additional land from Erwin.

On April 15, 1971, Howard sold the property to Robert G. Butzbach Jr. with the exception of a small tract he subdivided off for himself. Howard died on November 27, 1978.

Howard B. Corsa ran this ad for Moosehead Lodge in the 1948 *Moosehead Lake Gateway to Happiness* booklet. *Authors' collection.*

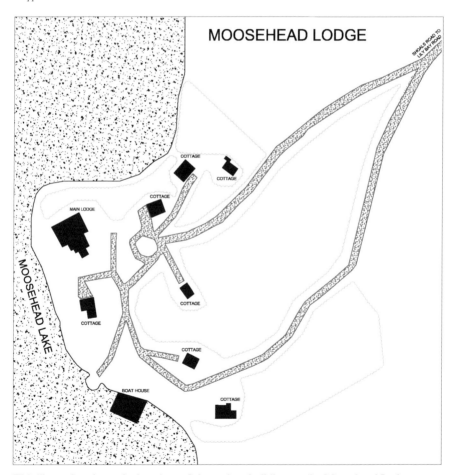

This illustration shows the locations of the various buildings at the Moosehead Lodge. *Illustration by Sean Billings.*

The Butzbaches continued to operate the Moosehead Lodge, advertising in *Field and Stream* in 1971 and 1972. Butzbach sold a portion of the property to Lutz N. and Waltraud A. Wallem on September 3, 1976; another portion on April 1, 1977; and the remainder of the land on August 26, 1977.

Despite the fact that the Wallems now owned it, Butzbach's Moosehead Lodge was advertised in the *Maine Guide to Camp & Cottage Rentals* in 1982 and 1985. The reason is unclear, but it is probably related to the fact that the Butzbaches held the mortgage on the property until 1988, when the Wallems paid it off.

The advertisements, which list Fay and Bob Butzbach as owners, make note of the availability of heated two-bedroom lakefront housekeeping cottages with paneling, insulation, carpeting and full modern kitchens and baths. Guests at these cottages had access to a private beach, dock, boat rentals and mooring facilities.

Not long after paying off the mortgage, the Wallems sold the property to Moosehead Lodge Realty Trust, George Gould, Trustee, on April 4, 1988. In October 1989, Gould hired Patrick Jackson to draw up a plan to subdivide the property separating the individual cottages on separate lots. Gould then sold it to the Second Maine Realty Corp. on July 12, 1991. The Second Maine Realty Corp. sold off the lots individually as follows: lot 1 to George P. Schott on August 30, 1991; lot 2 to Donald P. and Christine H. Watson on August 19, 1991; lot 3 to Patrick C. Jackson on August 25, 1991; lot 4 to Robert S. Lefaver, Donald Hartford and Lisa Hartford on August 23, 1991; and lot 5 to William P. Atwood and Sandra M. Daggett on August 29, 1991. With the sale of the individual lots, the properties became private cottages.

Chapter 8

THE COTTAGES

The Cottages was a sporting camp located off Shoals Road on what is now Harmony Lane. On September 2, 1949, Sam H. and Harmony B. Cheyney purchased lots 1, 2, 3 and 4 from Erwin Sloper. They also bought a triangular-shaped property adjoining these lots, as shown on Plan 2 of the subdivision that Erwin Sloper had completed in 1948.

Sam was a native of California and retired from the U.S. Air Force as a colonel. He and Harmony were looking to open a sporting camp in California after he retired. They decided to open a camp at Moosehead Lake instead after a fishing trip to Allagash in 1947 and a stay at Moosehead Lake in July 1949.

The couple hired Jim Gregan to start building the main cottage and lodge room in September and moved into their own cottage. The May 26, 1950 edition of the *Moosehead Gazette* states that two housekeeping cottages were being completed at that time and two more would be finished by July. On October 17, 1950, the Cheyneys purchased additional property from Erwin Sloper, and on May 19, 1953, they purchased property from Carl Tornquist, giving them a total of a little more than 13.6 acres.

Harmony wrote an article for the February 2, 1952 edition of the *Moosehead Gazette* describing their first winter at Moosehead Lake. Previously, the couple had gone south to Texas for the winter, but they decided instead to stay that winter and build two more cottages right on the water. These most likely would have been cottages 5 and 6.

Before they could stay, though, they had to winter-proof their cottage and water system, including the pumphouse, which pumped water out of

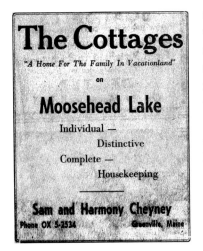

This ad for The Cottages is from the February 1956 *Moosehead Gazette.* Authors' collection.

the lake. The water lines were wrapped with heated electrical tape, a relatively new invention at the time. Harmony's article goes on to say that the water pump made it through temperatures of negative twenty-seven and they were comfortable.

In total, The Cottages would consist of eight housekeeping cottages and the main lodge. At some point, the main lodge was converted into a duplex, each side having a kitchen, bedroom, living room and bathroom. These were known as cottages 9 and 10. The Cheyneys ran The Cottages together until 1965, when Sam died. Harmony continued until 1976, when she retired to Florida. She died in 1991.

Harmony sold The Cottages to Frances M. Watson on February 17, 1977, and she and her husband, Earle, continued to run the site. The 1982 rate schedule shows cottages 1, 2, 3 and 4 renting for twenty-five dollars a night, with the rates for cottages 5 through 10 varying from twenty-seven dollars to thirty-four dollars. In the 1984 *Maine Guide to Camp & Cottage Rental*, The Cottages were advertised for twenty-nine to thirty-eight dollars a night with a three-night minimum. The ad also notes boats and motors were available for rent. Docking space, gas and oil were available, and there was a swimming beach that was safe for children.

In a plan titled "Shoal Road Acres," dated January 4, 1982, the Watsons subdivided The Cottages property into thirteen lots plus a residual lot of five acres. Cottages 1 through 9 were situated on lots with corresponding numbers. Plus, the plan created three additional vacant lots.

Even though the Watsons advertised cottages for rent through 1985, they began selling off lots one at a time in 1982. Lot 10, which had been vacant, was the first to change hands, selling on August 12, 1982, to Donald W. and Isabelle Moore, who owned land to the northeast of the lot already. Lot 12, also vacant, sold on September 24, 1982, to Robert J. Maciel.

In 1983, the first cottage lots were sold. On September 26, 1983, Paul G. Comba bought lot 8 and Thomas L. Young and Diane L. Allewalt purchased lot 5.

Lots continued to sell in 1984. Duane L. Brown and Lois M. Burns bought lot 6 on May 21, 1984. On July 3, 1984, Catherine A. Jorgensen bought lot

In this interior view, the fireplace in the main lodge at The Cottages can be seen shortly before the building was razed. Luckily, the fireplace was saved and will be incorporated into a new cottage to be built. *Courtesy Josh Wallace.*

A photo shows the main lodge at The Cottages as it looked in 2022, shortly before being razed due to structural issues. *Courtesy Josh Wallace.*

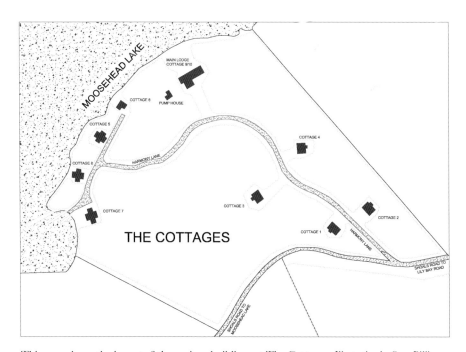

This map shows the layout of the various buildings at The Cottages. *Illustration by Sean Billings.*

7, and on September 20, 1984, David Wood bought lot 9, which contained the main lodge, then known as cottages 9 and 10. On October 26, 1984, Frank C. and Virginia Morang purchased lot 2.

Frances Watson continued to advertise cottage rentals as late as 1985, when she advertised four housekeeping cottages in that year's edition of *Maine Guide to Camp & Cottage Rentals*.

In 1985, the remaining cottage lots were sold. On January 18, 1985, Lawrence A. and Elizabeth C. Jacoinski purchased lot 1. John S. Symonds and Graham K. Bruder purchased lot 4 on July 1, 1985, and the last one, lot 3, was sold to William R. and Wendy S. Thorum on July 24, 1985.

Vacant lot 13 was sold to Millard H. and Cecilia T. Newell on July 21, 1986. The last parcel, the residual five-acre property, was sold to Kenneth P. and Peggy K. Beaulieu on October 27, 1987.

Cottage 6 was removed around 2009 to make way for a new cottage on the site. The main lodge was torn down in October 2022. Construction of a new cottage was started on the site in 2023.

Chapter 9

THE MOOSEHEAD LAKE HIGHLANDS

The Moosehead Lake Highlands is a development located on the western side of Lily Bay Road as you leave Greenville and start to climb Blair Hill. Lawrence K. Hall and his father, Pliny White Hall, began building it as a cottage development in 1926. Later, Lawrence's brother, Arthur, would also get involved.

Pliny was the superintendent of the Nelson & Hall Co. in Montgomery Center, Vermont, which made spruce butter tubs, butter boxes and candy pails out of veneer. His brother, Charles T. Hall, was the company president, and Charles E. Nelson was the vice president.

Census data from 1910 shows Pliny Hall, at age thirty-nine, living in Montgomery Center, Vermont, with his wife, Isabel E., age thirty-three, and sons Lawrence, age five, and Arthur, age two. Isabel's mother, Anna E. King, was also living with them at that time, according to the census. Pliny's wife, Elisabeth Isabel King, was born in Cherry Valley, Illinois, and died in 1917.

Pliny's brother, Charles, purchased the Veneer Box and Panel Company in Greenville after it went bankrupt in 1908. The February 3, 1910 edition of the *Piscataquis Observer* reports that Pliny Hall of Montgomery Center, Vermont, would be remaining in town for a while, installing tub machines in the veneer mill. That year, Pliny moved his family to Greenville so he could serve as the company superintendent. The *Piscataquis Observer*'s June 2, 1910 edition reports that Pliny had moved his family into the Clarence Tyler house on Cottage Street. Pliny purchased the house on August 13, 1910.

According to census data from 1920, the family continued to live in Greenville. The household included Pliny; his second wife, Grace; and his two children, Lawrence, age fifteen, and Arthur, age eleven. Additional information from the 1920 census indicates Pliny immigrated to the United States from Canada in 1886 and that he was naturalized as a citizen in 1891. It also says his father was born in New Hampshire and his mother in Vermont.

Pliny's son Lawrence King Hall was born on August 18, 1904, in Montgomery, Vermont. He attended Boston University and, in 1926, married Acelia Carey. She was born on December 24, 1905, in Philadelphia and grew up in Ocean City, New Jersey. She was the daughter of Timothy Jonathan and Nellie (Fenton) Carey and a graduate of the Virginia College for Women in Roanoke, Virginia.

Lawrence's brother, Arthur, attended the Taft School, a private preparatory school in Connecticut, in the mid-1920s and was on the football team as a guard. He went on to marry Ella T. Sloper, daughter of Harold and Carlotta Sloper. Arthur and Ella lived in Milton, Massachusetts, with their five-year-old daughter, Anna, according to 1940 census records. Arthur's occupation was listed as a teacher at a private school. The 1950 census lists the three of them along with another daughter, Jeanie, age four. Arthur's occupation was listed as an English teacher at an academy in the latter census.

Lawrence began working with his father on the Moosehead Lake Highlands development in 1926. Pliny purchased the initial tract of land in October of that year. Land transfers published in the November 4, 1926 *Piscataquis Observer* note the transfer, made from the H.M. Shaw Mfg. Co. to Pliny W. Hall, of a tract of land situated to the north of the southern line of the Saco Free Bridge grant and west of the Main Street (Lily Bay Road). The newspaper also included a land transfer of the Annie Young lot, which was part of lot 88 in the original Stanton survey, from E. Adaline Bigney to Pliny. Both of these lots were to become the Highlands.

In the plan for the Highlands, which was filed at the courthouse in 1927, Lawrence proposed approximately 750 cottage lots. Each lot was to be approximately five thousand square feet, or a little over a tenth of an acre. An article published in the May 28, 1927 issue of the *Bangor Daily News* says that although it was only started in late 1926, already more than 150 lots had sold. An ad from the June 4, 1927 edition of the *Bangor Daily News* calls the fifty-by-one-hundred-foot lots "big and roomy," with prices starting at $300.

The plan was drawn by J.D. Ring of Guilford and later modified by E.W. Vickery Jr. The roads in the development included Ridge Parkway, Fairmount Street, Sunset Avenue, Wayne Avenue, Highland Avenue and Pine Street, all of which came off present-day Lily Bay Road. Fairmount

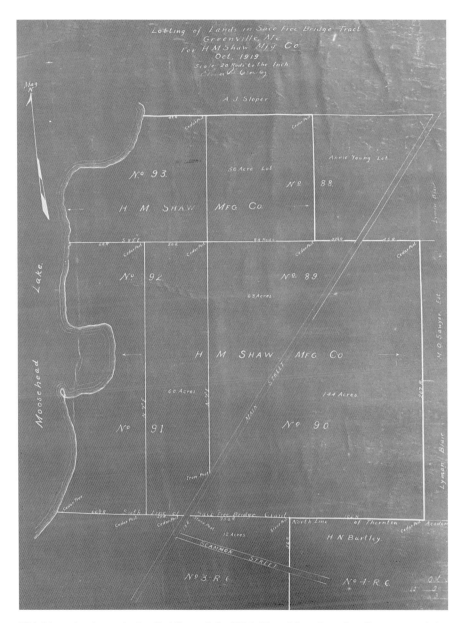

This blueprint shows the landholdings of the H.M. Shaw Manufacturing Company and the Annie Young lot in the Saco Free Bridge Tract of Greenville. Lots 88, 89, 90, 91, 92 and 93 were purchased by Pliny Hall and would become the location of the Moosehead Lake Highlands development. The northern corner of the Annie Young lot would become the location of the Sunset Motel. *Courtesy Piscataquis County Courthouse.*

Street does not currently exist, and Pine Street is now called Halls Avenue. The other roads exist as planned.

An ad in the June 4, 1927 edition of the *Bangor Daily News* states that Maine governor Ralph Owen Brewster would be talking about Moosehead Lake in his radio talk that evening at 9:00 p.m., broadcasting from WMAQ Chicago. People could listen to it and then take a drive up to visit the Moosehead Lake Highlands on Sunday. The ad states that the development was 350 acres in size.

Initially, Pliny transferred the land directly from himself to the buyer. Later, on May 22, 1929, Pliny transferred all the land to the Moosehead Lake Highlands, possibly in an effort to put Lawrence in control.

On September 18, 1929, the car Pliny and Grace were riding in was hit by a Maine Central train near Rockland, Maine. Pliny died instantly, and Grace died two days later at the Knox Memorial Hospital.

In 1930, Lawrence was still living in Greenville and serving as the president of a real estate corporation, according to census data. Living with him were his wife, Acelia P., and daughter, Nancy E. Census data also indicates that Acelia was born in Pennsylvania and that her father was born in Ireland and her mother in New Jersey.

By 1931, Lawrence had already built cottages on some of the lots in the development. A 1931 ad in the *Bangor Daily News* talks about people from Bangor who had found the cottages and log cabins to be an ideal weekend destination. For their time, the cottages and cabins were very modern, all being furnished and with running hot and cold artesian well water, ice, wood, electric and linens.

An August 15, 1934 ad in the *Bangor Daily News* states that the owners of the development were L.K. Hall and A.S. Hall, indicating that, at some point, Lawrence's brother, Arthur, had become involved. On December 8, 1938, all the land of the Moosehead Lake Highlands Inc. was transferred to Lawrence, according to deed book volume 260, page 469. The deed, signed by Arthur S. Hall as vice president, states that Lawrence was the owner of substantially all the outstanding stock of the Moosehead Lake Highlands Inc. and that it was about to be dissolved and liquidated. Lawrence borrowed $12,000 from his brother as a mortgage against much of the property, as shown in deed book volume 260, page 471. On January 12, 1939, he took an additional mortgage for $2,800 against lots in block 11 from Guilford Trust Company.

The 1940 census shows that Lawrence and Acelia Hall had started spending a portion of their time in the Ocean City, New Jersey area, where

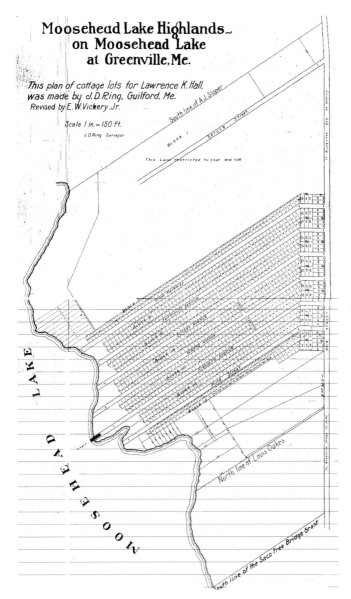

Moosehead Lake Highlands
on Moosehead Lake
at Greenville, Me.

This plan of cottage lots for Lawrence K. Hall
was made by J.D.Ring, Guilford, Me.
Revised by E.W.Vickery, Jr.

Scale 1 in. = 150 ft.
J.D.Ring Surveyor

This plan on file at the Piscataquis Courthouse shows the Moosehead Lake Highlands by J.D. Ring for Lawrence K. Hall. This plan was revised by E.W. Vickery Jr. and has the note "This Land restricted to cost and use." The original plan has a note that said, "This Tract to Be Divided into Lots." The original also did not show any lots to the north of Ridge Parkway. *Courtesy Piscataquis County Courthouse.*

they lived with their three children, Nancy E., Pliny W. and Lawrence K. Jr., all of whom were born in Greenville.

There was some excitement in the Halls' lives, according to a July 31, 1943 article in the *Bangor Daily News*. Titled "Big Bold Bear Raids Iceboxes in Greenville Area," the article states Clyde Whitney ended up shooting a three-hundred-pound bear in the yard of the cottage occupied by Mrs. Lawrence Hall and her three children.

Left: This ad for Lawrence K. Hall and the Highlands appeared in the 1948 *Moosehead Lake Gateway to Happiness. Authors' collection.*

Below: This postcard shows one of the cabins Lawrence Hall had for rent at the Moosehead Lake Highlands. *Authors' collection.*

The Big Log Cabin, located on the shore at Moosehead Lake Highlands, three bedrooms, two baths, living room, kitchen and large screened porch   Greenville, Maine

The 1947 *Moosehead Lake Gateway to Happiness* booklet contains advertisements stating the Highlands was in its twenty-first year, with housekeeping cottages and log cabins on the shore of Moosehead Lake. It also noted the cottages had electric ranges and refrigerators. Old town boats and canoes were available.

The 1950 census data indicates Lawrence and Acelia were living part of their time in Cape May County, New Jersey, with their sons, Pliny and Lawrence Jr. The elder Lawrence was working as a house painter, and Pliny, at age nineteen, was a carpenter. Lawrence Jr. was in school.

Lawrence Sr. was also a pilot and ran a seaplane service at the Highlands. His obituary states that he was a member of the Silver Wings Association of Old Time Pilots. The August 29, 1936 issue of the *Bangor Daily News* includes an ad for the Maine Lakes Air Service Inc., located at Moosehead Highlands. The company used a Robin monoplane equipped with Edo pontoons with a 9–1 gliding ratio, according to the ad.

This postcard provides an interior view of the Big Log Cabin that Lawrence Hall had for rent at the Moosehead Lake Highlands. *Authors' collection.*

This is another one of the cottages Lawrence Hall had for rent at the Moosehead Highlands. *Authors' collection.*

COMMUNITY HOUSE AT MOOSEHEAD LAKE HIGHLANDS
GREENVILLE, MAINE

Left: The Community House at the Moosehead Lake Highlands was a gathering and meeting place for the residents who owned cottages in the development. *Authors' collection.*

Below: This postcard shows the Harvey Lodge and Resthaven. The Harvey Lodge was owned by Orville C. and Faith B. Harvey. Orville was an undertaker in Greenville. Resthaven was owned by Dr. and Mrs. Charles Brooks of South Portland. Many of the postcards of the time listed the Coffee House on them even though they were not owned by the Barney's Moosehead Coffee House. Being located on the main road, the coffeehouse had a lot of name recognition and most likely was the main place to purchase the postcards. *Copy from the original negative, authors' collection, now in the Moosehead Historical Society Collection.*

Cottages   Coffee House   Greenville Maine

Nick Hanson's CAMPS

Moosehead Highlands

This ad for Nick Hanson's Camps, located in the Moosehead Highlands, appears in the 1948 *Moosehead Lake Gateway to Happiness. Authors' collection.*

In 1965, Lawrence was still advertising the Highlands, including cottages and boats for rent. Ads note it was close to Squaw Mountain Ski Area.

The Halls weren't the only ones to build and rent cottages at the Highlands. Nick Hanson's Camps were advertised in the 1947 *Moosehead Lake Gateway to Happiness*. His ad lists cabins that were completely equipped for housekeeping with two bedrooms, a living room, a kitchenette, electric and wood stoves, a refrigerator and running water.

John H. Brown of J.H. Brown's Insurance ran a group known as Brown's Cottages. They were located 150 yards from the Community House, dock and swimming beach. The Community House was a small building located near the beach that served as a meeting place for the residents who owned and rented cottages in the Highlands. Advertised as complete, the cottages featured three bedrooms, including one with a double bed, one with twin beds and one with a single bed. The cottages also included a bathroom; kitchen; living room with a Franklin fireplace and a studio couch; and screened porch with glider and chairs. Appliances included an electric range and refrigerator, water heater, radio, percolator and toaster. Plus, the cottages were furnished with good wool blankets, bed linens and towels and state-analyzed artesian well water.

Mayton Housekeeping Cottages were owned by Robert Mayhew. He advertised two new cottages in 1947 plus three cottages that were previously owned by Paul D. Sanders. Humphrey's Camps and Murray's Cottages were among the others advertised in the Highlands.

Lawrence K. Hall died on December 13, 1984, and the Highlands properties went to his wife, Acelia. Lawrence had been a charter member and past president of the Greenville Chamber of Commerce and a Mason at the

Above: This ad, from the July 26, 1963 *Moosehead Gazette*, lists the many options and services offered by Lawrence K. Hall and the Moosehead Lake Highlands. *Authors' collection.*

Opposite, left: This is the front of a brochure for Brown's Cottage in the Moosehead Lake Highlands. *Collection of the Moosehead Historical Society.*

Opposite, right: This ad for Murray's Cottages in the Moosehead Lake Highlands appears in the February 1956 issue of the *Moosehead Gazette. Authors' collection.*

Columbia-Doric. During World War II, he worked at naval installations as a civilian, possibly at the Lakehurst Air Force Base in New Jersey doing work on radio towers. Acelia Hall died on October 24, 1992, and the property was passed down to the Halls' children. Acelia was a member of the Ready Worker Society, the Daughters of the American Revolution and the Maine Historical Society, as well as being a past president of the board of directors of the Shaw Public Library.

Chapter 10

THE MOOSEHEAD COFFEE HOUSE

What is now an overgrown lot along Lily Bay Road was once the site of the former Quartucci's North Woods Inn, an Italian American restaurant. Before that, the site was home to the Moosehead Coffee House and Overnight Camps, which got their start as part of the Moosehead Lake Highlands development.

The land between the streets had been designated by block and section numbers as part of the Moosehead Lake Highlands development. Edith M. Barney purchased lots 46, 47 and 48 in Block 11, Section A; lot 55 in Block 11, Section B; lots 49, 50, 51 and 52 in Block 10, Section A; and lots 56, 58, 61, 63 and 65 in Block 10, Section B. The coffee house was located in Block 10, Section A, lots 50, 51 and 52. These lots faced Lily Bay Road, giving Edith access to potential customers from both the development and passing traffic. The other lots were used for cabins. An ad in the June 14, 1930 edition of the *Bangor Daily News* even mentions that the Moosehead Coffee House and Overnight Camps are on the direct route to the Ripogenus Dam.

A 1927 news clipping in the Moosehead Historical Society archives reports that Edith had a crew laying the foundation for a public dining room to cost $5,000 and that a fine well had been sunk. The November 23, 1927 issue of the *Bangor Daily News* states that the outside of the Moosehead Coffee House was complete and that it offered a wonderful view of Moosehead Lake. At that time, the trees between the road and the lake had been cut back and not regrown to the extent they are today. A 1928 article in the Moosehead Historical Society archives reports that the restaurant opened for business

Edith M. Barney owned the Moosehead Coffee House when the photo for this postcard view was taken. The coffee house also sold gasoline, and the Gulf gasoline pumps can be seen out front. *Authors' collection.*

with dining in a screened front porch and sun parlor, each big enough to seat sixty people. The rooms were attractively furnished with dainty ivory finished tables and chairs painted in bright colors that harmonized with the draperies. At that time, Mrs. Marguerite Kinney was in charge of cooking and Elaine Bartley and Ruth Duty were waitresses. Other articles state a four-car garage was in the process of being built and two overnight cottages were completed. Two gas tanks were planned for in front of the coffee house.

The May 19, 1939 issue of the *Bangor Daily News* reports that the coffee house opened for the season on May 15 with Edith Barney managing, Wayne Hussey and his wife in charge of the dining room and kitchen and Muriel Huggard of Houlton and Faye Gregan of Greenville employed as waitresses.

Edith and her husband, Lawrence, eventually built a total of eleven cabins to be rented out. Five had kitchens and bathrooms, and three of these were half-log construction. Five were one-room cabins with attached baths. The others were frame construction. The Barneys lived in the log cabin located on lots 46 and 47 in Block 11, Section A, on Lily Bay Road.

Lawrence died on April 19, 1946, leaving Edith to operate the coffee house alone. On June 17, 1953, she sold the property to Howard R. "Dutchie" and Doris E. Murray. According to the Piscataquis County

Adirondack chairs sit on the lawn for guests to use at the Moosehead Coffee House. This photo postcard shows the southern side of the building. *Copy from the original negative, authors' collection, now in the Moosehead Historical Society Collection.*

This cottage, located to the left of the Moosehead Coffee House, was the first one built by the Barneys. They lived in it until other buildings were completed. Known as the Barney Camp, it still stands. *Copy from the original negative, authors' collection, now in the Moosehead Historical Society Collection.*

This postcard shows the inside of the Moosehead Coffee House porch. *Authors' collection.*

deed book, volume 311, page 172, the Murrays purchased lot 48 in Block 11, Section A; lot 55 in Block 11, Section B; lots 49, 50, 51 and 52 in Block 10, Section A; and lots 56, 58, 61, 63 and 65 in Block 10, Section B. Edith kept lots 46 and 47 in Block 11, Section A, which included the log cabin in which she lived.

At this time, the Murrays operated Murray's Cabins at Center Cove in Greenville, near the Masonic temple, and the agreement was that Edith would stay and operate the coffee house. That agreement didn't last long because she died on December 17, 1953. The Murrays decided to sell their camp on Center Cove and concentrate on running the coffee house. The Murrays had previously operated the Log Cabin Restaurant, the Aeroplane Diner and variety stores in Greenville and Greenville Junction.

When Edith died, her niece, Marguerite A. Kinney, became the owner of lots 46 and 47 in Block 11, Section A, which included the log cabin where Edith had lived. On November 14, 1956, Marguerite sold those lots to Howard R. Murray. The Murrays then moved into the log cabin located on lots 46 and 47.

When the Murrays operated the coffee house and cabins, Doris ran the kitchen and Howard did maintenance. In 1961, the Murrays contacted Joseph Quartucci of New Jersey, who had been coming up to the coffee house cabins since 1950. He was also friends with both Edith Barney and

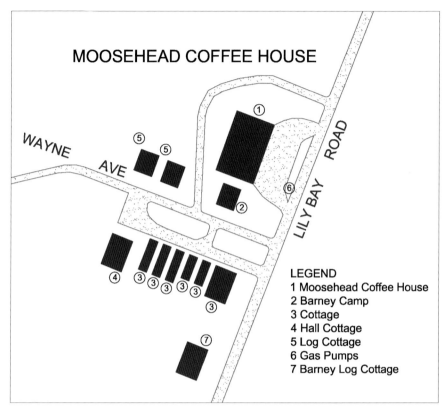

This map shows the location of the Moosehead Coffee House and its cottages along Wayne Avenue at the intersection of Lily Bay Road. *Illustration by Sean Billings.*

the Murrays. The Murrays knew that Quartucci loved the coffee house and wanted to know if he wanted to purchase it.

Quartucci and his wife, Gloria, had no experience running a restaurant and were unsure if they would be able to do it. Joseph was a reporter for a newspaper in Paterson, New Jersey, and Gloria was a Linotype operator for a paper in Fair Lawn, New Jersey. As a result, the Murrays agreed to lease the restaurant to the Quartuccis for the 1961 season and continue to operate the cabins.

After the season ended, the Quartuccis decided to purchase the restaurant, and the sale was recorded on June 23, 1962. Documents can be found in deed book volume 345, page 244. The Murrays also sold lots 50 and 51 and portions of 49 and 52 in Block 10, Section A, to the Quartuccis, who changed the name of the restaurant to Quartucci's North Woods Inn.

The Moosehead Coffee House cottage can be seen on the right in this postcard view looking up Wayne Avenue. The coffee house, which was located off to the left, is not seen in the photo. *Copy from the original negative, authors' collection, now in the Moosehead Historical Society Collection.*

Looking from the parking lot at the front of the Moosehead Coffee House, cottages can be seen across Wayne Avenue in this postcard view. *Copy from the original negative, authors' collection, now in the Moosehead Historical Society Collection.*

Looking down Wayne Avenue at a turn in the road, the cottages can be seen on the left and Resthaven on the right. *Copy from the original negative, authors' collection, now in the Moosehead Historical Society Collection.*

This log cabin, one of several that was located on Wayne Avenue next to the Barney Camp, still stands today. *Authors' collection.*

North Woods Inn
Restaurant & Cabins
Lily Bay Road — Greenville
OPEN 7 A. M. TO 10 P. M. EVERY DAY
FORMERLY MOOSEHEAD COFFEE HOUSE

Italian - American Food
Prop. Joe & Gloria Quartucci

This ad for Quartucci's North Woods Inn appears in the July 26, 1963 issue of the *Moosehead Gazette. Authors' collection.*

In 1963, the Quartuccis decided to purchase some of the cabins from the Murrays, as shown in the county deed books. On May 15, 1963, the Murrays sold lot 48 in Block 11, Section A; lot 55 in Block 11, Section B; and part of lot 49 in Block 10, Section A, reserving the right to take water from the well on lot 49, according to deed book volume 345, page 439. These lots contained the cabins. The Murrays retained ownership of part of lot 52, as well as a cabin on lots 56 and 58, a cabin on the eastern half of lot 49 and a cabin on lots 61, 63 and 65. The Quartuccis purchased what remained of lot 52 in Block 10, Section A, as shown in deed book volume 359, page 321, dated September 21, 1968.

The Quartuccis purchased lots 46 and 47 in Block 11, Section A, from the Murrays on August 4, 1971, according to deed book volume 398, page 165.

On December 14, 1967, the Murrays sold the cabin on lots 56 and 58 to Lancy Christie, as shown in deed book volume 371, page 481. On June 17, 1965, the Murrays sold the cabin on the eastern half of lot 49 to John Files, as shown in deed book volume 365, page 328. The cabin on lots 61, 63 and 65 was sold on March 30, 1971, to Maxim Squiers, as per deed book volume 390, page 495.

Quartucci sold the cabin on lot 55 to Mathias Bolton on June 1, 1985, according to deed book volume 704, page 246.

The Quartuccis operated the North Woods Inn until 1976, when the building was torn down. The lot remains empty. Joseph Quartucci died in November 2009. Lots 50, 51 and 52 (where the coffee house stood) and lots 46, 47, 48 and part of 49 (where some original cabins still stand) were owned by the Quartuccis' son, Chris, until 2010. In that year, he transferred lots 50, 51 and portions of 49 and 52 to his son Nicholas A. Quartucci and lots 46, 47 and 48 to his son Michael A. Quartucci. Chris Quartucci died on April 24, 2021. The Quartucci family still owns the property and cottages.

Chapter 11

THE SUNSET LODGE

The Sunset Lodge, also known as the Sunset Motel, was located on the west side of Lily Bay on Blair Hill next to the Macfarlane property and on the northern part of Lawrence K. Hall's Moosehead Lake Highlands property. It contained a main lodge that still stands with five cabins around it.

Lawrence K. Hall's plan for the Moosehead Lake Highlands showed development only for lots in the southern half of his landholdings. These lots were concentrated in the area from Halls Avenue to Ridge Parkway, but the property extended northward up to what was then the Sloper property, formerly the Macfarlane property. Toward the northern end of Hall's property, there was a note that said, "This Tract to Be Divided into Lots." When the plan was revised, a proposed road called Spruce Street was shown on the Moosehead Lake Highlands plan, and a note was added on the northern area of the plan around Spruce Street that states, "This land restricted to cost and use." Possibly he agreed to limit the development in the northern section to get the high-density development that he proposed in the Highlands.

Fred B. Mullen purchased the northwest corner of this lot and built a cottage on the property. On December 1, 1932, Moosehead Lake Highlands Inc., with Lawrence K. Hall as president, sold a piece of land at the far northern end, bordering the Sloper and Mullen properties, to George and Katheryn Barmore, as shown in deed book volume 242, page 429. The Barmores then purchased the land and cottage from Fred B. Mullen on April 30, 1934, as described in deed book volume 245, page 366. The deed

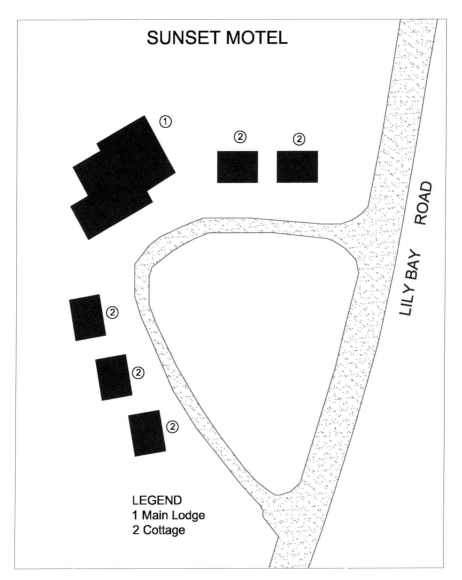

The locations of the main lodge and cabins of the Sunset Motel are seen here. The cabins were removed in 1965, but the main lodge still stands. *Illustration by Sean Billings.*

to the property referenced that this was part of the property purchased by Pliny W. Hall from E. Adeline Bigney on October 13, 1926. The *Piscataquis Observer* reports on June 21, 1934, that the Barmores of Princeton, New Jersey, were staying at the Mullen cottage, which they had purchased. The January 16, 1936 edition of the *Piscataquis Observer* reports that the Barmores had returned to the Mullen cottage after a short visit to New Jersey and that they had recently registered as residents of Greenville.

The Barmores owned the property until February 13, 1941, when they sold it to William A. and Eva White Barraclough, as recorded in the courthouse in deed book volume 270, page 226. There is no mention of cabins in the deed at this point, and it seems the Barmores used it as a private cottage.

The *Piscataquis Observer*'s September 10, 1942 issue reports that the Maquaso Club held the first meeting of the season with a 7:00 p.m. dinner at the Sunset Lodge. This seems to be the first reference to the lodge being used for anything other than a private residence. The June 28, 1945 issue of the *Piscataquis Observer* reports that the wedding supper of Ruth D. Hamlin and Maurice Anderson was held at the Sunset Lodge following their wedding at the Union Church.

The Barracloughs owned the Sunset Lodge until May 16, 1946, when they sold it to Carl and Edith Tornquist, as recorded in the deed book volume 284, page 248. The deed states the transfer was for the land together with all cabins, seeming to indicate that the Barracloughs were the first to make the lodge into a commercial business. The Sunset Lodge was the first house the Tornquists bought when moving to Greenville before building a home on the Scammon farm, as described in chapter 1. The Tornquists' granddaughter Prudy Tornquist Richards said she does not believe they ran the Sunset Lodge as a business but rather used it only as a residence.

Ralph and Dorothy Bartlett purchased the property and the buildings from Carl and Edith Tornquist on September 1, 1953. The Bartletts operated Sunset Motel, consisting of the main lodge, one large housekeeping cottage and four sleeping cabins. They also ran an antique shop at the location. In the September 7, 1962 edition of the *Moosehead Gazette*, it was advertised as Bartlett's Log Motel with an antique and gift shop on location. In the July 26, 1963 edition of the *Moosehead Gazette*, it was advertised as the Sunset Motel.

The February 1966 edition of the *Moosehead Gazette* reports that in August 1965, the Bartletts decided to retire and sell the entire motel and antique shop. An auction was scheduled for August 30, but before it could take place, Leroy Edwards, who owned the Blair Mansion across the street from the Sunset Motel, purchased the property. The property and lodge were sold to Edwards on September 28, 1965.

As part of the sale, Leroy and Bernice Edwards let the Bartletts keep the housekeeping cottage and the four cabins as long as they were moved off the property. Ronald Wortman purchased the housekeeping cottage and moved it off site. Joseph W. Cartwright of Guilford purchased two of the cabins

Top: The Bartletts were referring to the Sunset Lodge as Bartlett's Log Motel, as seen in this ad from the September 7, 1962 *Moosehead Gazette. Authors' collection.*

Bottom: The Bartletts referred to the inn as the Sunset Motel in this ad from the July 26, 1963 *Moosehead Gazette. Authors' collection.*

and had Manley Haley of Guilford move them to lots leased from Scott Paper near Squaw Mountain Ski Area. John Sanborn of Dover-Foxcroft and Donald C. Templet of Guilford each purchased a cabin and also had them moved to the Scott Paper property.

The Edwardses owned the property for a few years, but only the lodge remained after all the cabins were removed. On October 15, 1969, the Edwardses sold it to Oscar A. and Lana H. Gagnon. The deed contained conditions and restrictions so the property could not be used as a motel again. It stipulated that only a private dwelling could be situated on the property and that the premises could not be used for trade, manufacture, business or as a place of public resort. Before purchasing the Sunset Lodge, Oscar was the chief warden for the Maine Forest Service for the Chesuncook District, located at Chesuncook Dam, and Lana was a schoolteacher at Chesuncook. Oscar later became a district ranger for the Greenville District.

The Gagnons owned the Sunset Lodge until November 1, 1985, when it was sold to Clifford and Beverly Trembley and Robert Tremblay. Robert Tremblay became the sole owner on March 31, 2017, and still owns it.

BIBLIOGRAPHY

BOOKS

Colby, George N. *Atlas of Piscataquis County, Maine.* Houlton, ME: George N. Colby & Co., 1882.

Farrar, Charles A.J. *Farrar's Illustrated Guide Book to Moosehead Lake.* Boston: Lee and Shepard, 1879.

———. *Farrar's Illustrated Guide Book to Moosehead Lake.* Boston: Lee and Shepard, 1884.

Moffatt, Frederick C. *The Travels of James and Emma Cameron, 1840–1900: Paintbrush for Hire.* Knoxville: University of Tennessee Press, 2018.

Smith, Mac. *Mainers on the Titanic.* Essex, CT: Down East Books, 2014.

Steele, Thomas Sedgwick. *Canoe and Camera: A Two Hundred Mile Tour Through the Maine Forests.* New York: Orange Judd Company, 1880.

True, Emma J. *100 Years on Moosehead Lake, History of Greenville.* Augusta, ME: Augusta Press, 1936.

Way, John M., Jr. *Guide to Moosehead Lake and Northern Maine.* Boston: Bradford & Anthony, 1874.

U.S. CENSUS

1850. Town of Southampton, Connecticut, October 28, 1850.

1850. Township of Yonkers, New York, page 201, September 5, 1850.

1860. Town of Greenville, Maine, page 4, June 1, 1860.

1860. Town of New Britain, Connecticut, page 47, June 13, 1860.

1860. Town of Yonkers, New York, page 97, June 15, 1860.

1870. Third Ward of Chicago, Illinois, page 184, July 7, 1870.

1870. Town of New Britain, Connecticut, page 103, July 14, 1870.

1870. Town of New Britain, Connecticut, page 107, July 16, 1870.

1880. Greenville and Territory North, Maine, Supervisor's District No. 2, Enumeration District No. 72, June 1880.

1880. Town of New Britain, Connecticut, Supervisor's District No. 2, Enumeration District No. 21, page 13, June 4, 1880.

1880. Town of New Britain, Connecticut, Supervisor's District No. 2, Enumeration District No. 23, page 1, June 1, 1880.

1900. Greenville, Maine, Supervisor's District No 110, Enumeration District No. 133, June 5, 1900.

1900. New Brunswick, New Jersey, Supervisor's District No. 4, Enumeration District No. 46, sheet 16, June 15, 1900.

1900. Town of New Britain, Connecticut, Supervisor's District No. 26, Enumeration District No. 207, sheet 2, June 1, 1900.

1900. Town of New Britain, Connecticut, Supervisor's District No. 26, Enumeration District No. 207, sheet 5, June 4–5, 1900.

1910. Greenville, Maine, Supervisor's District 2, Enumeration District No. 201, sheet 14, April 30, 1910.

1910. Montgomery, Vermont, Supervisor's District No. 3, Enumeration District No. 100, sheet 7A, April 30, 1910.

1910. Town of New Britain, Connecticut, Supervisor's District No. 29, Enumeration District No. 224, sheet 7, April 19, 1910.

1910. Wilton, Connecticut, Supervisor's District No. 29, Enumeration District No. 125, April 27, 1910.

1920. Greenville, Maine, Supervisor's District No. 4, Enumeration District No. 134, page 2B, January 3–5, 1920.

1920. Greenville, Maine, Supervisor's District No. 4, Enumeration District No. 134, page 45, January 5–6, 1920.

1920. Town of New Britain, Connecticut, Supervisor's District No. 1, Enumeration District No. 144, sheet 4, January 3, 1920.

1920. Town of New Britain, Connecticut, Supervisor's District No. 1, Enumeration District No. 152, sheet 3A, January 2, 1920.

1920. Wilton, Connecticut, Supervisor's District 2d, Enumeration District No. 184, sheet 11B, January 26, 1920.

1930. Greenville, Maine, Supervisor's District No. 2, Enumeration District No. 11-20, sheet 11A, April 25, 1930.

1930. Greenville, Maine, Supervisor's District No. 2, Enumeration District No. 11-20, sheet 15B, April 30, 1930.

1930. Piscataway Township, New Jersey, Supervisor's District No. 10, Enumeration District No. 12-97, sheet 8B, April 14, 1930.

1930. Town of New Britain, Connecticut, Supervisor's District No. 2, Enumeration District No. 2-160, sheet 1B, April 2, 1930.

1930. Town of New Britain, Connecticut, Supervisor's District No. 2, Enumeration District No. 2-172, sheet 2A-B, April 3, 1930.

1940. Greenville, Maine, Supervisor's District No. 3, Enumeration District No. 11-16, sheet 12A, April 23, 1940.

1940. Milton, Massachusetts, Supervisor's District No. 13, Enumeration District No. 11-135, sheet 1A, April 2, 1940.

1940. Ocean City, New Jersey, Supervisor's District No. 2, Enumeration District No. 5-22, sheet 1A, April 2, 1940.

1940. Pima, Arizona, Supervisor's District No. 3, Enumeration District No. 10-39, sheet 6B, April 28 and 29, 1940.

1940. Town of New Britain, Connecticut, Supervisor's District No. 1, Enumeration District No. 2-120, sheet 3B, April 6, 1940.

1950. Milton, Massachusetts, Enumeration District No. 11-240, sheet 10, April 15, 1950.

1950. Ocean City, New Jersey, Supervisor's District No. 5-22, sheet 37, May 2, 1950.

1950. Town of New Britain, Connecticut, Enumeration District No. 11-30, sheet 7, April 6, 1950.

1950. Wilton, Connecticut, Enumeration District No. 1-312, sheet 17, April 19, 1950.

NEWSPAPER ARTICLES AND JOURNALS

Bangor Daily News

"Big Bold Bear Raids Iceboxes in Greenville Area." July 31, 1943.

"Doris E. 'Dot' Murray Obituary." January 1, 1994.

"Fine Cows at Hillside Farm." November 21, 1914.

"Greenville Happenings of Interest to the Residents of This Vicinity." June 18, 1930.

"Lawrence Barney, Moosehead Coffee House Owner, Dies." April 20, 1946.

"Pansies Picked in Lyman Blair's Garden on Sunday." November 19, 1935.

"Tourists Flock to Coffee House." August 1, 1931.

"Will Raise Some Mule-Foot Hogs." December 12, 1914.

Piscataquis Observer [Dover, ME]

"Greenslope on Blair's Hill." July 2, 1936.

"Kineo Street Railway." March 27, 1903.

Mills, Shirley. "News of Towns in Western Piscataquis County." October 13, 1892.

———. "News of Towns in Western Piscataquis County." October 22, 1896.

———. "News of Towns in Western Piscataquis County." April 1, 1897.

———. "News of Towns in Western Piscataquis County." June 29, 1899.

"Mrs. Zarrina N. Macfarlane obituary," April 30, 1903.

"News of Towns in Western Piscataquis County, Greenville." March 23, 1899.

"News of Towns in Western Piscataquis County, Greenville." July 1, 1909.

"News of Towns in Western Piscataquis County, Greenville." April 24, 1913.

"News of Towns in Western Piscataquis County, Greenville." November 27, 1913.

"News of Towns in Western Piscataquis County, Greenville." November 9, 1916.

"News of Towns in Western Piscataquis County, Greenville." July 5, 1917.

"News of Towns in Western Piscataquis County, Greenville." October 11, 1917.

"News of Towns in Western Piscataquis County, Greenville." September 22, 1921.

"News of Towns in Western Piscataquis County, Greenville." September 29, 1921.

"News of Towns in Western Piscataquis County, Greenville." November 17, 1921.

"News of Towns in Western Piscataquis County, Greenville." August 13, 1925.

"News of Towns in Western Piscataquis County, Greenville." October 21, 1926.

"News of Towns in Western Piscataquis County, Greenville." December 10, 1931.

"News of Towns in Western Piscataquis County, Greenville." January 16, 1936.

"News of Towns in Western Piscataquis County, Greenville." July 19, 1936.

"News of Towns in Western Piscataquis County, Greenville." January 12, 1950.

"News of Towns in Western Piscataquis County, Greenville." November 19, 1953.

"News of Towns in Western Piscataquis County, Greenville." April 22, 1954.

"News of Towns in Western Piscataquis County, Greenville." February 23, 1956.

"News of Towns in Western Piscataquis County, Greenville." August 1, 1963.

"News of Towns in Western Piscataquis County, Greenville." June 6, 1968.

"News of Towns in Western Piscataquis County, Greenville." May 28, 1970.

"Notice of Foreclosure, Victor W. Macfarlane." October 17, 1907.

"Piscataquis Real Estate Conveyances, Andrew J. Sloper et. al. to Roberta J. Nicholas." September 3, 1925.

"Real Estate Transfers, Victor W. Macfarlane to Robert W. Johnson." November 22, 1906.

"Real Estate Transfers, William T. Sloper to Andrew J. Sloper et al." September 20, 1917.

Other

Bachelder, Peter D. "1982 Maine Guide to Camp and Cottage Rentals." *Maine Publicity Bureau.* 1982.

———. "1985 Maine Guide to Camp and Cottage Rentals," *Maine Publicity Bureau.* 1985.

Sprague, John Francis. "Victor Wells Macfarlane." *Sprague's Journal of Maine History* 6, no. 3 (1913): 101–2.

Land Plans

Plan, final subdivision plan Grand View Estates. By GVS Surveying and Land Services, Inc. June 10, 2006.

Plan of Greenville, Piscataquis County, 1878.

Plan of House Lots for Erwin W. Sloper. Plans 1–4, by E.J. and G.B. Smith, on file at Piscataquis County Courthouse. August 11, 1948, vol. 5, page 25.

Plan of Moosehead Heights Subdivision. By Kelley Engineering. December 9, 1987, Cab. H, No. 283.

Plan of Moosehead Lake Highlands. Plan of Cottage Lots for Lawrence K. Hall, by J.D. Ring, surveyor, on file Piscataquis County Courthouse. January 1, 1926, vol. 3, page 46.

Plan of Moosehead Lake Highlands. Plan of Cottage Lots for Lawrence K. Hall, by J.D. Ring, surveyor, on file Piscataquis County Courthouse. September 1, 1927, vol. 3, page 50.

Plan of Moosehead Lake Highlands. Plan of Cottage Lots for Lawrence K. Hall, by J.D. Ring, surveyor. Revised by E.W. Vickery Jr., on file Piscataquis County Courthouse. July 13, 1949, vol. 5, page 28.

Plan of Moosehead Lake Highlands. Plan of Cottage Lots for Lawrence K. Hall, by J.D. Ring, surveyor. Revised by E.W. Vickery Jr., on file Piscataquis County Courthouse. August 3, 1949, vol. 5, page 29.

Plan of Moosehead Lake Properties. By Main-Land Development Consultants, Inc. November 3, 1986, Cab. H, No 163.

Plan of Moosehead Lodge Subdivision. By Kelley Construction Engineering, Inc. October 1989, Cab. J, No. 91.

Plan of Property Conveyed to Lutz N. Wallem by Robert G. Butzbach Jr. By Norman Chase. August 4, 1976, Cab. B, No. 199.

Plan of Shoal Road Acres. By Main-Land Development Consultants, Inc. January 4, 1982.

Plan of Sloper Property, Blair Hill. By Forrest Whitman on file Piscataquis County Courthouse. December 12, 1984, vol. H, page 40.

Plan of Sloper-Wallem Subdivision. By Main-Land Development Consultants, on file Piscataquis County Courthouse. September 10, 1985, vol. H, page 79.

Plan showing addition to Norman P. Cooley Lot. E.W. Vickery, surveyor. October 19, 1946.

Plan showing details of the various land owned by George H. Thompson, et al. By Forrest G. Whitman. August 8, 1980. Cab. F, No. 190.

Plan showing Lands of H.M. Shaw Mfg. Co. located in the Saco Free Bridge Tract. Drawn by Elmer Crowley, October 1919.

Plan showing Nicholas and Johnson property. August 18, 1925. Deed Book vol. 223, page 235.

Plan showing part of the Bernice B. Edwards Property located on the west side of Lily Bay Road. By Forrest G. Whitman. May 14, 1977, Cab. F, No. 13.

Plan showing property lines of May F. Butterworth. By Forrest G. Whitman. July 18, 1982.

Plan, survey of land owned by James Fitzpatrick. By Norman Chase. October 10, 1973.

DEEDS

Robert Scammon to Edmund Scammon, July 31, 1837, vol. 1, page 466.

Samuel Scammon to Edmund Scammon, April 24, 1854, vol. 31, page 52.

Edmund Scammon to James Cameron, September 12, 1865, vol. 44, page 524.

Mary Scammon to Edmund Scammon, September 12, 1865, vol. 44, page 523.

Emma S. Cameron, wife of Reverend James Cameron, to Victor Macfarlane, July 3, 1872, vol. 59, page 505.

Mortgage, Victor Macfarlane to Emma Cameron, July 3, 1872, vol. 63, page 11.

Zanina Macfarlane to Cornelia Blair, September 29, 1892, vol. 112, page 314.

Victor W. and Zanina Macfarlane to Andrew J. Sloper, August 22, 1896, vol. 122, page 333.

Victor and Zanina Macfarlane to Lyman Blair, September 29, 1896, vol. 120, page 202.

E. Adaline Bigney to Lyman Blair, June 27, 1901, vol. 134, page 222.

Victor Macfarlane to Veneer Box and Panel Co., December 4, 1905, vol. 154, page 80.

Victor Macfarlane to Robert Johnson, October 29, 1906, vol. 155, page 301.

Victor Macfarlane to Cornelia Blair, April 2, 1907, vol. 156, page 47.

Victor Macfarlane to Robert Johnson, September 23, 1908, vol. 164, page 50.

Victor Macfarlane to Robert Johnson, November 19, 1908, vol. 164, page 172.

Clarence Tyler to Pliny Hall, August 13, 1910, vol. 173, page 322.

Anna Varney to Lyman Blair, January 8, 1915, vol. 186, page 319.

Victor Macfarlane to Cornelia Blair, August 14, 1915, vol. 187, page 80.

Victor Macfarlane to Cornelia Blair, August 14, 1915, vol. 187, page 97.

Victor Macfarlane to Andrew J. Harold T. and William T. Sloper, August 25, 1915, vol. 184, page 277.

Andrew J. Sloper to Myra Sloper, October 6, 1917, vol. 217, page 175.

H.M. Shaw Manufacturing Co. to Pliny Hall, October 26, 1920, vol. 213, page 245.

Lyman Blair to Thomas Hoops, July 2, 1924, vol. 218, page 244.

Roberta J. Nicholas to Andrew J. and Harold T. Sloper, August 12, 1925, vol. 223, page 233.

H.M. Shaw Manufacturing Co. to Pliny Hall, October 1, 1926, vol. 224, page 452.

E. Adaline Bigney, Fred Bigney, Mary Scammon, Sadie Mayo and Mabel Hunt to Pliny Hall, October 13, 1926, vol. 224, page 453.

Pliny Hall to Mrs. Laurence P. Barney, July 14, 1927, vol. 227, page 349.

Pliny Hall to Mrs. Laurence P. Barney, September 6, 1927, vol. 227, page 465.

Pliny Hall to Mrs. Laurence P. Barney, December 21, 1927, vol. 229, page 84.

Pliny Hall to Edith M. Barney, April 1, 1929, vol. 235, page 175.

Pliny Hall to Moosehead Lake Highlands, May 22, 1929, vol. 234, page 154.

Merrill Trust Co. Trustee to Moosehead Lake Highlands, October 14, 1930, vol. 236, page 272.

Lyman Blair to Norman P. Cooley, October 29, 1930, vol. 236, page 282.

Moosehead Lake Highlands, Inc., Lawrence K. Hall, President, to Edith M. Barney, November 16, 1931, vol. 242, page 86.

Moosehead Lake Highlands, Inc., Lawrence K. Hall, President, to George and Kathryn Barmore, December 1, 1932, vol. 242, page 429.

Moosehead Lake Highlands to Lawrence K. Hall, December 8, 1938, vol. 260, page 469.

George and Kathryn Barmore to William A. and Eva White Barraclough, February 13, 1941, vol. 270, page 226.

Roberta Johnson Nicholas to Howard B. Corsa, October 15, 1942, vol. 203, page 152.

Roberta Johnson Nicholas to Howard B. Corsa, October 15, 1942, vol. 203, page 153.

Carlotta Sloper, Emily Sloper and Ella Sloper Hall to Carlotta C. Sloper, November 28, 1945, vol. 283, page 465.

William A. and Eva White Barraclough to Carl A. and Edith S. Tornquist, May 15, 1946, vol. 284, page 248.

Erwin W. Sloper to Howard Corsa, November 25, 1946, vol. 285, page 121.

Erwin W. Sloper to Carl A. Tornquist, June 7, 1947, vol. 289, page 33.

Erwin W. Sloper to Isaac and Amie G. Nelson, August 15, 1947, vol. 288, page 311.

Erwin W. Sloper to Robert Diehl, September 6, 1947, vol. 288, page 416.

Cyrus H. and Mary S. Adams to Norman P. Cooley, November 9, 1947, vol. 285, page 30.

Erwin W. Sloper to Ralph E. Anderson, January 27, 1948, vol. 292, page 131.

Erwin W. Sloper to T. Stephen Runcy, July 3, 1948, vol. 305, page 478.

Carlotta C. Sloper to Erwin W. Sloper, October 1, 1948, vol. 286, page 476.

Erwin W. Sloper to Sam W. and Harmony B. Cheyney, September 2, 1949, vol. 300, page 235.

Myra W. Sloper to George H. Thompson, September 6, 1950, vol. 301, page 351.

Erwin W. Sloper to Sam W. and Harmony B. Cheyney, October 17, 1950, vol. 301, page 459.

Erwin W. Sloper to Carl A. Tornquist, January 15, 1951, vol. 304, page 264.

Erwin W. Sloper to Carl A. Tornquist, January 15, 1951, vol. 304, page 265.

Erwin W. Sloper to Howard B. Corsa, February 20, 1951, vol. 304, page 101.

Erwin W. Sloper to Alban J. and Shirbie M. Pelletier, September 20, 1951, vol. 305, page 30.

T. Stephen Runcy to George Thompson, June 27, 1952, vol. 310, page 64.

Erwin W. Sloper to Myra Sloper, August 8, 1952, vol. 310, page 427.

Erwin W. Sloper to Myra W. Sloper, February 2, 1953, vol. 310, page 445.

Carl A. Tornquist to Sam W. and Harmony B. Cheyney, May 19, 1953, vol. 311, page 98.

Edith M. Barney to Howard R. and Doris E. Murray, June 17, 1953, vol. 311, page 172.

Alban J. and Shirbie M. Pelletier to John and Edna Dyer, July 22, 1953, vol. 311, page 221.

Carl A. and Edith S. Tornquist to Ralph H. and Dorothy A. Bartlett, September 1, 1953, vol. 311, page 340.

Robert S. Ludwig to Vaughn L. and Ruth B. Simpson, May 12, 1954, vol. 316, page 239.

Erwin W. Sloper to Ralph E. Anderson, August 15, 1955, vol. 317, page 491.

Erwin W. Sloper to Vaughn L. and Ruth B. Simpson, September 10, 1955, vol. 322, page 84.

Robert M. Diehl to Vaughn L. and Ruth B. Simpson, September 21, 1955, vol. 322, page 83.

Carl A. Tornquist to John F. and Edna Dyer, December 2, 1955, vol. 322, page 223.

John and Edna Dyer to Millard I. and Lillian M. Elsemore, June 6, 1956, vol. 327, page 44.

Marguerite A. Kinney to Howard R. Murray, November 14, 1956, vol. 323, page 241.

Myra W. Sloper to Daniel F. and Helen J. Ancona, August 30, 1957, vol. 325, page 348.

Carl A. Tornquist to John W. and Ann G. Tornquist, August 7, 1958, vol. 327, page 483.

Erwin W. Sloper to Lawrence Rowe, October 28, 1958, vol. 335, page 219.

John W. Tornquist to Clarence A. and Ruth A. Lang, April 28, 1959, vol. 336, page 90.

Cyrus H. Adams to Leroy P. and Bernice Edwards, July 18, 1960, vol. 336, page 352.

Ralph E. and Muriel L. Anderson to Glenys G. Pero, November 10, 1960, vol. 338, page 97.

Ralph E. Anderson to Richard O. and Glenys G. Pero, April 18, 1961, vol. 345, page 3.

Howard R. and Doris E. Murray to Joseph and Gloria A. Quartucci, June 23, 1962, vol. 345, page 244.

Howard R. and Doris E. Murray to Joseph and Gloria A. Quartucci, May 15, 1963, vol. 345, page 439.

John F. and Edna Dyer to Thomas S. and Elinor Runcy, July 18, 1963, vol. 345, page 474.

Carl A. Tornquist to Clarence A. and Ruth A. Lang, July 19, 1963, vol. 345, page 473.

Lawrence K. Hall to Leroy P. and Bernice B. Edwards, August 8, 1963, vol. 348, page 411.

Lawrence O. Rowe to Daniel F. Ancona Jr., September 20, 1965, vol. 350, page 393.

Daniel F. Ancona Jr. to Morton and Jill R. Malkin, September 23, 1965, vol. 359, page 95.

Ralph H. and Dorothy A. Bartlett to Leroy P. and Bernice B. Edwards, September 28, 1965, vol. 359, page 67.

Morton and Jill R. Malkin to Lawrence O. Rowe, November 22, 1965, vol. 350, page 448.

Erwin W. Sloper to Daniel F. Ancona Jr., January 16, 1966, vol. 360, page 130.

Carl A. and Edith S. Tornquist to Herbert and Thelma M. Cochrane, November 21, 1966, vol. 365, page 366.

Millard I. Elsemore to Clyde F. and Estelle M. Morton, August 21, 1967, vol. 371, page 259.

Leroy P. and Bernice B. Edwards to Oscar A. and Lana H. Gagnon, October 15, 1969, vol, 383, page 261.

Vaughn L. Simpson to Karl W. and Nancy E. Watler, June 17, 1970, vol. 386, page 175.

Thomas S. and Elinor Runcy to Edward J. and Nancy E. Eggert, August 27, 1970, vol. 390, page 231.

Helen J. Ancona to Daniel S. and Eva B. Gurney, November 13, 1970, vol. 387, page 363.

Lawrence Rowe to Karl W. and Nancy E. Watler, January 6, 1971, vol. 390, page 417.

Lawrence Rowe to James E. and Patricia M. Fitz-Patrick, January 14, 1971, vol. 387, page 386.

Howard B. Corsa to Robert G. Butzbach Jr., April 15, 1971, vol. 387, page 453.

Howard R. Murray to Joseph and Gloria Quartucci, July 31, 1971, vol. 398, page 165.

Samuel Auerbach to Karl W. and Nancy E. Watler, September 14, 1972, vol. 396, page 436.

Glenys G. Pero to Karl W. and Nancy E. Watler, October 16, 1973, vol. 413, page 399.

Robert G. Butzbach Jr. to Lutz N. and Waltraud A. Wallem, September 3, 1976, vol. 447, page 139.

Harmony B. Cheyney to Frances M. Watson, February 17, 1977, vol. 453, page 424.

Robert G. Butzbach Jr. to Lutz N. and Waltraud A. Wallem, August 27, 1977, vol. 459, page 443.

Bernice B. Edwards to Carl S. Zuendel, September 9, 1977, vol. 460, page 487.

Daniel S. and Eva B. Gurney to Lutz N. and Waltraud A. Wallem, March 15, 1978, vol. 466, page 173.

Lutz N. and Waltraud A. Wallem to Ruth M. Cool and James S. Devlin, August 31, 1978, vol. 474, page 137.

Bernice B. Edwards to James Hilton, September 14, 1978, vol. 474, page 393.

Glenys G. Pero to Carl G. and Dorothy M. Vogelman, December 27, 1979, vol. 492, page 424.

Charles O. Keirstead to Carl G. and Dorothy M. Vogelman, January 10, 1980, vol. 492, page 422.

Harmony B. Cheyney to Earle W. and Frances M. Watson, January 17, 1980, vol. 491, page 457.

Frances M. Watson to Donald W. and Isabelle M. Moore, August 12, 1982, vol. 529, page 418.

Frances N. and Earle W. Watson to Robert J. Maciel, September 24, 1982, vol. 531, page 264.

Frances N. and Earle W. Watson to Paul G. Comba, September 26, 1983, vol. 549, page 488.

Frances N. and Earle W. Watson to Thomas L. Young and Diane L. Allewalt, September 26, 1983, vol. 550, page 310.

May F. Butterworth to May F. Butterworth and Ruth B. Ecker, February 28, 1984, vol. 555, page 313.

Ralph E. and Muriel L. Anderson to Daniel and Janice E. Hanscome, February 28, 1984, vol. 555, page 449.

Frances N. and Earle W. Watson to Duane L. Brown and Lois M. Burns, May 21, 1984, vol. 562, page 48.

Frances N. and Earle W. Watson to Catherine A. Jorgensen, July 3, 1984, vol. 560, page 319.

Frances N. And Earle W. Watson to Catherine A. Jorgensen, July 3, 1984, vol. 560, page 321.

Frances N. and Earle W. Watson to David D. Wood, September 20, 1984, vol. 568, page 268.

Frances N. and Earle W. Watson to Frank C. and Virginia Morang, October 26, 1984, vol. 569, page 244.

Frances N. and Earle W. Watson to Lawrence A. and Elizabeth Jacoinski, January 18, 1985, vol. 572, page 128.

Peter S. and Margaret C. Vole to Karl W. and Nancy E. Watler, June 17, 1985, vol. 581, page 406.

Frances N. and Earle W. Watson to John S. Symonds and Graham K. Bruder, July 1, 1985, vol. 582, page 204.

Frances N. and Earle W. Watson to William R. and Wendy S. Thorum, July 24, 1985, vol. 583, page 449.

Oscar A. and Beatrice A. Gagnon to Clifford and Beverly Trembley and Robert Tremblay, November 1, 1985, vol. 591, page 78.

Ruth M. Devlin (Cool) and James S. Devlin to Jerry Horger Anderson and James D. Anderson, December 16, 1985, vol. 593, page 146.

Clarence A. and Ruth A. Lang to Shirley Noyes and David D. Lang, February 25, 1986, vol. 597, page 2.

Frances N. and Earle W. Watson to Millard H. and Cecilia T. Newell, July 21, 1986, vol. 603, page 423.

James E. Fitz-Patrick to Wayne C. Shaw, September 16, 1986, vol. 619, page 50.

T. Stephen Runcy to Thomas S. and Elinor Runcy, September 30, 1986, vol. 659, page 119.

Lutz N. and Waltraud A. Wallem to Devlin Corporation, January 8, 1987, vol. 625, page 265.

Frances N. and Earle W. Watson to Kenneth P. and Peggy K. Beaulieu, October 27, 1987, vol. 663, page 55.

Devlin Corporation to John M. Goodwin, January 19, 1988, vol. 666, page 264.

Devlin Corporation to K.O.A. Inc., January 19, 1988, vol. 666, page 266.

John M. Goodwin to K.O.A. Inc., February 5, 1988, vol. 668, page 228.

Lutz N. and Waltraud A. Wallem to Moosehead Lodge Realty Trust, George R. Gould Trustee, April 4, 1988, vol. 674, page 146.

John M. Goodwin to K.O.A. Inc., December 30, 1988, vol. 708, page 278.

K.O.A. Inc., to George R. Gould Jr. and Deborah Johnson, December 30, 1988, vol. 708, page 288.

Winifred H. Corsa to Howard B. Corsa Jr., November 31, 1989, vol. 754, page 174.

Bernice B. Edwards to Kenneth F. and Mary K. Hughes, July 30, 1990, vol. 778, page 340.

Amy Nelson to Craig H. Nelson and Ina Jane Gerow, November 9, 1990, vol. 791, page 142.

Jerry Horger Anderson and James D. Anderson to Roger S. and Jennifer A. Cauchi, March 11, 1991, vol. 832, page 16.

George R. Gould, Trustee of the Moosehead Lodge Realty Trust to Second Maine Realty Corp., July 12, 1991, vol. 814, page 197.

George R. Gould Jr. and Deborah Johnson to George R. Gould Sr., August 2, 1991, vol. 819, page 303.

Ruth B. Ecker to Ruth B. Ecker, Cheryl E. Hohman, Julia Hohman, Todd Homan, August 22, 1991, vol. 820, page 164.

Second Maine Realty Corp. to Robert S. Lefaver Jr., Robert S. Lefaver Sr., Donald Hartford and Lisa Hartford, August 23, 1991, vol. 820, page 306.

Second Maine Realty Corp. to Patrick C. Jackson, August 25, 1991, vol. 821, page 53.

Second Maine Realty Corp. to William P. Atwood and Sandra M. Daggett, August 29, 1991, vol. 821, page 252.

Second Maine Realty Corp. to George P. Schott, August 30, 1991, vol. 822, page 30.

Second Maine Realty Corp. to Donald P. and Christine H. Watson, September 19, 1991, vol. 824, page 80.

George R. Gould to Lisette Fauteux, January 4, 1993, vol. 890, page 239.

Elinor Runcy to Elinor, Stephen R.T. Runcy and Elinor Bette Walsh, July 9, 1993, vol. 902, page 173.

Kenneth F. and Mary K. Hughes to Ruth Ecker, July 27, 1993, vol. 905, page 317.

Clyde F. and Estelle M. Morton to Michael E. and Ellen L. Jobin, October 21, 1993, vol. 916, page 168.

Kenneth F. and Mary K. Hughes to Ellen L. Jobin, October 7, 1994, vol. 959, page 59.

Carl G. and Dorothy M. Vogelman to Christian R. Picker, May 18, 1995, vol. 987, page 40.

James E. Fitz-Patrick to Roger S. and Jennifer Cauchi, May 8, 1996, vol. 1029, page 234.

Edward J. Eggert to Michael Jobin, May 22, 1997, vol. 1080, page 350.

Ellen L. Jobin to Daniel J. and Ruth E. McLaughlin, November 25, 1997, vol. 1108, page 37.

Shirley Noyes and David D. Lang to Roger E. and Carol G. Mills, April 8, 1999, vol. 1191, page 304.

Craig H. Nelson and Ina Jane Gerow to William K. Blackford, April 23, 2001, vol. 1309, page 74.

Roger S. and Jennifer A. Cauchi to Bruce and Sonda Hamilton, June 22, 2001, vol. 1320, page 83.

Roger E. and Carol G. Mills to Vikki L. and Charles K. Ryder, June 29, 2001, vol. 1321, page 275.

Christian R. Picker to Dorinda S. Galbraith, December 23, 2004, vol. 1631, page 45.

Vikki L. and Charles K. Ryder to Grace M. Bardsley, May 26, 2005, vol. 1654, page 208.

Estate of Herbert Cochrane to Warren H. Cochrane, July 14, 2006, vol. 1803, page 198.

Ellen Byrd Jobin to Nancy Wescott, July 20, 2006, vol. 1764, page 242.

Cheryl E, Hohman, Julia Hohman Brightbill, Todd W. Hohman to Debbie B. Stankauskas, September 2, 2006, vol. 1777, page 144.

Dorinda S. Galbraith to Dana A. and Amy R. Bishop, September 29, 2006, vol. 1783, page 244.

Bruce and Sonda Hamilton to Lakeview Lodging Inc., May 30, 2007, vol. 1843, page 4.

Warren H. Cockrane to Warren H. Cockrane and Linda A. Koski, July 27, 2007, vol. 1860, page 313.

Duane L. Brown and Lois Marie Deady-Schultz f/n/a Lois M. Burns to Edward and Arlene Jewett, September 19, 2008, vol. 1946, page 67.

Bank of New York to Christiana Trust, April 15, 2016, vol. 2425, page 97.

Arns Inc. to Shatosha Inc., April 18, 2016, vol. 2425, page 101.

Christiana Trust to Arns Inc., April 19, 2016, vol. 2425, page 99.

Clifford, Beverly Trembley and Robert Tremblay to Robert Tremblay, March 31, 2017, vol. 2488, page 114.

Lisette Y. Fauteux to Stephen G. Foster, December 21, 2017, vol. 2532, page 95.

Debbie B. Stankauskas to Sheehan Gallager, March 14, 2019, vol. 2610, page 240.

Nancy A. Wescott to Sean D. and Johanna S. Billings, July 10, 2020, vol. 2693, page 194.

Linda J. and Dennis D. Bortis (Lakeview Lodging Inc.) to Highlands Lodging, Inc., March 22, 2021, vol. 2757, page 192.

Grace M. Bardsley to Robert E. Tracy, July 1, 2021, vol. 2782, page 82.

Grace M. Bardsley to Sean D. and Johanna S. Billings, July 21, 2021, vol. 2786, page 284.

Robert E. Tracy to Eastern Property, LLC, September 8, 2021, vol. 2798, page 234.

Eastern Property, LLC to Jennifer M. Whitlow Revocable Trust, March 14, 2022, vol. 2838, page 131.

Daniel J. and Ruth E. McLaughlin to Blair Hill Inn LLC, April 15, 2022, vol. 2843, page 19.

Right of Way Dedications

Right of Way Dedication, Erwin W. Sloper to public, June 6, 1956, vol. 324, page 140.

Right of Way Dedication, Lawrence O. Rowe to present and future lot owners of Horizons West, access to Moosehead Lake over lot 6, Plan 3, March 14, 1966, vol. 361, page 360.

Right of Way Dedication, Moosehead Lake Access, Rowe to Horizons West lot owners, March 14, 1966, vol. 361 page 360.

Wills

Abstract of Will of Norman P. Cooley, November 12, 1953, vol. 4, page 391.

Abstract of Will of Zanina Macfarlane, July 7, 1903, vol. 2, page 79.

Websites

Hart & Cooley. www.hartandcooley.com.

ABOUT THE AUTHORS

Sean D. Billings is licensed as a professional engineer in Maine and Pennsylvania. He received his bachelor's degree in engineering technology from Temple University. Although he has worked as an engineer for more than thirty years, he is a historian at heart. He has been involved in historical societies for the last twenty-five years and is currently a trustee for the Moosehead Historical Society. Previously, he resurrected the defunct Steuben Historical Society in Washington County, Maine, and served as its president for three years. He was also a founding member of the Lehigh Township Historical Society in Pennsylvania, serving as its president for ten years.

He is the author of the books *Incline Planes of Pennsylvania* and *Dieter's Foundry*, and his articles on Smith Brothers glass and Mount Washington art glass have been published in *AntiqueWeek*.

Johanna S. Billings is an award-winning writer, editor and photographer. She worked for newspapers in both Pennsylvania and Maine and covered the antiques trade for local, regional and national publications. Her work has also appeared in national magazines including *Redbook*, *Reader's Digest* and *Cat Fancy*. She has since retired from publishing and now runs The Lily Cat: North Woods Antiques and Buttons in Monson, Maine, a business she and Sean launched in 2020. Johanna received her bachelor's degree in English summa cum laude from Gwynedd Mercy College in Gwynedd Valley, Pennsylvania.

Together, Sean and Johanna have coauthored several books. Among them are *Petit Manan Land Company Near Bar Harbor, Maine: The Making of a National Wildlife Refuge* (Fonthill Media, America Through Time Series, 2020), *Lehigh Township* (Arcadia Publishing, Images of America Series, 2002), *Indian Trail and Edgemont Amusement Parks* (Arcadia Publishing, Images of America Series, 2005), *Slatington, Walnutport and Washington Township* (Arcadia Publishing, Images of America Series, 2006), *Wyoming County* (Arcadia Publishing, Postcard History Series, 2004) and two books on antique art glass, *Collectible Glass Rose Bowls* (Antique Trader Books, 1999) and *Peachblow Glass* (Krause Publications, 2001). The two also coauthored the paper "Colorful Sands: Glassmaking and the Peachblow Craze," presented at the 2001 Canal History and Technology Symposium in Easton, Pennsylvania.

The couple has one adult daughter, Kayleigh. They live in Greenville with their four cats.